LESSONS LEARNED

Successful Management in the Changing Marketplace

RADE B. VUKMIR

Dichotomy Press
Sewickley, PA

Copyright © 2003, 2015
Rade B. Vukmir

Dichotomy Press
www.dichotomypress.com

Sewickley
Pennsylvania 15143

All Rights Reserved
Printed in the United States of America

Lessons Learned: Successful Management in the Changing Marketplace

Library of Congress Control Number: 2015917578

ISBN: 978-1-944351-03-8 (Hardcover)
ISBN: 978-1-944351-04-5 (Paperback)
eISBN: 978-1-944351-05-2 (Electronic)

No part of this publication may be reproduced, stored in a retrieval system, or transmitted in any form or by any means electronic, mechanical, photocopying, recording, or otherwise, without the written permission of the author or publisher.

Contents

Preface	v
Chapter 1. Introduction	1
2. History	5
3. Business Start-Up	9
4. Public Relations	13
5. Leadership	17
6. Personnel Development	23
7. Managerial Development	27
8. Business Models	37
9. Success	49
10. Competition	59
11. Crisis Management	65
12. Employer Stressors	71
13. Employee Development	85
14. Best "Business Practice" Companies	97
15. Prologue	105
16. Conclusion	107
Index	109
About the Author	119

Preface

"An honest day's work for a good day's pay."

T. D. Duckworth,
Jones & Laughlin Steel Co.

This simple admonition has served as a rational business model, whether dealing with an industrial blue-collar employee or in the cybertech intellectual property arena.

I encountered this simplistic, but elegant business philosophy as a summer employee working in a steel mill in Aliquippa, Pennsylvania, where the model served to help finance college tuition and subsequent medical school. This work ethic pervaded the clinical practice as a medical trainee, and subsequent practice of emergency medicine and as a critical care physician.

Much time was spent laboring in the intensive care unit caring for the critically ill from medical illness or trauma. Interspersed with this activity was time spent in the emergency department caring for those with significant injuries, worsening of chronic health conditions or pediatric illness. Here, one third of the time is spent ministering to the psychosocial needs of elders, adults and children.

Next, a degree in law helped me to understand and compete in an ever-changing market. Understanding the rules of the game allowed one to continue on hopefully a proper path, while balancing work product and fair compensation.

Lastly, the most important lessons were learned at home in the formative years from my Mother-Leni, Father-Matthew, and Grandparents-Rade and Anka who were each responsible for their own immigrant success story. They tried to succeed at all costs—my grandparents, selling canned good and my mother, operating a coffee business to supplement their incomes as factory workers. Finally, this monodimensional work product is softened and improved by Alisa, and the focused determination of my sister, Alana.

The secret of success is based on equal portions of hard work and "burning desire."

Chapter 1

Introduction

Albert Einstein had succinctly incorporated three rules of work into his day-to-day life. First, out of clutter, find simplicity; second from discord, find harmony; and third in the middle of difficulty lies opportunity.[1] Change in most circumstances is clearly anxiety producing, but offers tremendous opportunity for growth and development for those who anticipate and relish this opportunity.

Einstein's Three Rules of Work
1. Out of clutter, find simplicity.
2. From discord, find harmony.
3. In difficulty lies opportunity.

Adapted from 1

Overall, the potential for improvement should help to accentuate the work product, as well as create new opportunities for growth and novel business development using hard work and the "bright shining path" as your moral model.

However, a frequently encountered approach is to "modify the truth" or more commonly known as the "Why People Lie" concept described by Michael C. Jensen of the Monitor Group.[2] He suggests monitoring for the "credibility gap," which has become an "acceptable" managerial tool in troubled times; where the gaming of sales, targets and time frames for budgetary review gives the appearance of achieving goals. The appropriate management strategy to address this issue is not to tell employees "don't lie," but to eliminate the use of budget targets in compensation formulas. If the worker is forced to make difficult choices between honest behavior and an extraordinary proportion of their compensation, the choice will be self-evident.

Why People Lie
1. Credibility Gap
2. Gaming Targets, Revenue, Time Periods
3. Appearance of Achieving Goals

Adapted from 2

The business world is replete with stories of both success and failure acknowledging and analyzing problems on the basis of continual improvement. A prominent global telecommunications company found its stock stable during telecom run-up in the 1990's. Kessler provided an analysis of potential reasons for this phenomenon, which he calls "The Seven Deadly Sins."[3] First, avoid nepotism. Nothing has good talent running for the hills faster than promoting from within based on genetics. Second, not all technology needs to be invented within—sometimes both the pace and effectiveness of a new technology is accentuated with co-promotion.

Third, the surefire way to failure is to compete with your own customers. It is a certainty that end users are extremely resistant to competition from their supplier. Fourth, never confuse manufacturing with innovation. Attributes that translate into ease of manufacturing do not necessarily translate into ease of usability for the consumer.

Fifth, vertical integration is helpful, but horizontal integration selling components and other services to outsiders can be profitable as well. Sixth, perhaps the greatest sin is failing to leverage the brand. Some companies are industry cornerstones with names synonymous with the industry. However, at some point, marketing will be necessary to maintain predominance, don't miss the transition.

Lastly, don't just hide in high end. Consumers will continue to search for efficient low cost products. Don't be left with quality high end with no entry-level products available to the consumer.

"The Seven Deadly Sins"
1. Avoid nepotism.
2. Innovation is nice but not necessary.
3. Don't compete with your customers.
4. Don't think manufacturing is innovation.
5. Don't forsake horizontal integration.
6. Avoid failure to leverage the brand.
7. Don't just hide in the high end.

Adapted from 3

Therefore, the best approach to a successful business practice is to try to manage expectations, which may be best achieved by being able to underpromise and yet overdeliver. This goal of managing realistic expectations allows the best chance of operational success.

The optimum method to achieve this goal is to align incentives—both positive and negative reinforcement for all personnel involved in the product or service delivery line using customer satisfaction as the quality performance monitor.

References

1. Einstein, Albert. *Ideas and Opinions*. Bonanza Books, Reprint 1988.
2. Jensen, M. C.: Managers Journal: Why People Lie. *Wall Street Journal*, New York, NY; 8 January 2001.
3. Kessler, Andy. "Motorola's Seven Deadly Sins." *Wall Street Journal*. 22 January 2001.

Chapter 2

History

Modern businesses should review *Lessons Learned* for a perspective on past entrepreneurs' successes and failures. Looking to New York City, boasting the largest accumulation of business intelligencia in the world, allows one to examine the traits of its century-old, closely held family business contingent. Daniel Gross reports on the collection of such enterprises from a pictorial exhibit at the New York Historical Society entitled "Family Matters: Century-Old New York Businesses."[1]

First, they sought to carve out a small niche and stick to it doggedly in a focused way. There was no attempt to dominate the market, provide a vast comprehensive array of services to a huge number of clients, nor compete for a spot on the Fortune 500 List.

Peter Gougelman emigrated from Switzerland in 1851 as an ocularist who created eye prosthesis and passed this talent on to his sons, Pierre and Paul, as well as their descendants. This ongoing specialty concern has a long list of clients including such luminaries as Helen Keller and Jose Feliciano.

Likewise, Henry Mali moved from Belgium in 1826 and continued his knitting trade as Henry W. T. Mali and Company. They specialized in making the green cloth used to surface pool tables. Secondly, when they chose to expand it was to a related enterprise, as Frederick Mali began to manufacture pool cues in 1960.

Thirdly, successive transfer of an ongoing business concern is likely if descendants attempt to blend their own personnel interest into new business areas. This concern is embodied in a business concern established in 1899 by a 19-year-old entrepreneur DeWitt H. Stern working as an insurance broker. Subsequently, his son DeWitt A. Stern, who had a love of coin and stamp collecting, expanded the company to insure his and other valuable numismatic collections.

Likewise, the next generation found Jolyon Stern whose passion for the theater directed the concern to insure theatre productions and stars for major Broadway shows such as *Cats* and *The Wiz*.

Fourth, understanding the use of new technology is a key to survival. New technology firms are not usually associated with multi-generational operation, except for companies such as Motorola and Corning. Jacob Starr an immigrant metal worker from the Ukraine in 1890 began to work for a sign company began by Benjamin Strauss. Starr became interested in a new technology—electricity—and left in 1920 to start his own firm—ArtKraft—that dealt with neon, a new sign illumination substance. This enterprise merged with Strauss, his original employer in 1935 to illuminate the "Great White Way." His granddaughter Tama continues the tradition of lighting up Broadway, including the Times Square New Year's Eve Ball Drop.

Fifth, almost universally, multi-generational businesses are relatively small in comparison, but are preserved by the familial survival instinct that triumphs in an adverse market. In 1892, Antonio Ferdada operated an Italian pastry shop on Grand Street a century before biscotti and macchiato became trendy café accompaniments.

Lessons of Century-Old Companies

1. Defines a small focused niche and defend doggedly.
2. Expand to a related enterprise.
3. Blend personal interests to related business lines.
4. Understanding the use of new technology is a key to survival.
5. Familial small businesses tend to survive based on the self-preservation instinct.
6. Change with the times.

Adapted from 1

These family businesses certainly capitalized on New World opportunities. However, they must change with the times. In 1852, Frank Winfield Woolworth began his first store in Lancaster, Pennsylvania rising to over 1,000 "five and dime stores." Unfortunately, the trend progressed away from this retail marketing strategy and the last "five and ten store" closed recently.

References

1. Gross, Daniel: All in the Family. *Attache*; April 2002:15-16.

Chapter 3

Business Start-Up

Although this is not meant to be a business primer, it is useful to review the business start-up process. Henry Wang, principal of I. Venture Lab, a technology think tank, suggests the four "P" principle.[1] This principle stresses 1. A focus on *people*, 2. The goal of remaining *passionate* about your business, 3. Having a *purpose* for what you are doing, and 4. Finding the right *partners* as the keys to a successful business venture.

The Four P's
1. Focus on *people*
2. Remain *passionate*
3. Have a *purpose*
4. Right *partners*

Adapted from 1

Perhaps, an unstated "P" is the *property* component of intellectual property—the idea. This concept may clearly be the most valuable commodity in any business plan and should be closely guarded and protected by the entrepreneur.

A successful business plan model has been offered and summarized by Jim Hopkins.[2] It is suggested that the three most significant errors encountered in the business start-up process are first, to not have a cogent written business plan at all. This is perhaps the most crucial aspect of new or existing business development and operation. Secondly, to only need a business plan to get a bank loan. Clearly, even operational concerns are best served by an annual revision of their business plans, especially in the rapidly changing marketplace.

Thirdly, they may feel that the plan does not need to be written since they know it so intimately well. Although the last contention may be true, the best way to ensure success is to inculcate the knowledge and passion of the leader into every employee by sharing the corporate mission actualized into a written model that can be best understood by employees in this written format.

Business Plan Keys

1. Develop prior to opening the enterprise
2. Write yourself
3. Review and revise
4. Use outside consultant
5. Five year time frame

Adapted from 2

The model suggested to develop this business plan involves a logical step-wise approach.[2] First, you should develop the plan before you open the business. Second, write the plan yourself since only you have the special passion for your business. However, you should acknowledge the need for specialized assistance if necessary. Third, you should regularly review and revise the plan. Establish a quarterly, semiannual, or annual assessment plan to keep the business on track. Fourth, consider hiring an outside consultant, lawyer, or accountant to both obtain expert advice on navigating difficult waters, and to obtain a fresh outside perspective. Lastly, this plan should have a definitive time frame. It is probably unrealistic to look beyond a five-year period in business cycles.

Plan Format

1. Length of 12-100 pages
2. Executive summary
3. Business description
4. Market place
5. Management
6. Financial

Adapted from 2

Good companies come and go, but you can hold on much past the prime of some ideas and products. Try to find a manual typewriter or the Beta video format these days.

Then, to summarize an effective business plan development; Step One, it is not just about the money to finance the concept, it is about developing an effective operating plan.[2] Step Two, consider outside consultants, but not at the sake of doing your own research utilizing either the library or web, depending on your skill set.

Step Three, getting down to details, finds a document with a recommended length of 12 to 100 pages beginning with an executive summary, and including a description of your business, an analysis of the market place, the management, personnel, profile tools to deal with change, and your financial resources and funding plan.

Lastly, Step Four, suggests that once completed you should leap into action with your plan, don't just put it on the shelf. Time is of the essence in today's changing business environment and your maximal impact on the economic environment is most certainly sensitive to the passage of time.

The cornerstone of any new business is the employer himself or herself. In this business climate managers clearly have more power than employees do in a wide variety of economic and geographic areas. The balance between labor and management is consistently shifting and dependent on the economic climate and local work force availability.

Perhaps, this concept is best stated by Barbara Bridger, Vice President of Human Resources, Butler Manufacturing of Kansas City, Missouri. "If you don't treat your employees right, you can't service your customers."[3]

Clearly, the best value is afforded when there is a level playing field with balance between management and worker power, ensuring an adequate worker supply and demand and market driven compensation that manifests as aligned business objectives for all participants in the endeavor.

References

1. Wang, Henry. "War Stories: Follow Five P's and Think Positively about Local Start-Ups." *Pittsburgh Post Gazette*, 13 July 2000.

2. Hopkins, Jim. "Entrepreneurs 101: Chart Your Firm's Route before Hitting the Road." *USA Today*, 9 November 2000.
3. Hymowitz, Carol. "In The Lead: Managers are Starting to Gain More Clout over Their Employees." *Wall Street Journal*, 30 January 2001.

Chapter 4

Public Relations

The key to business success is a positive customer or client interaction. This is a pervasive universal concept borrowing from the healthcare model in that there are really three customers; the actual purchaser of goods or services, peers or co-workers, as well as management ultimately; according to James M. Johnson MD, PhD, President and CEO of Emergency Consultants, Inc., an emergency medicine management firm.[1]

Public relation skills have a wide range of applications. Most simply in formal business conversation, one should inquire about the client or superior's life or career. The ability to refocus the conversation to "their story" rather than yours is a tremendously successful negotiation tool according to Alisa Zimmel, District Sales Manager, Takeda Pharmaceuticals Co.[2]

An extensive amount of discussion involves interpersonal relations and interpreting human behavior by maximizing observation skills. "Body language doesn't lie, because people don't realize they are doing it" offered Jimmy Cvetic, a retired policeman who spent a career reading subtleties of human interaction.[3] Bill Acheson, national lecturer, claims a 70% accuracy rate in interpretation of nonverbal clues correlated to the actual intent of the conversant.

In fact, the business world has it's own "interrogation" sessions each day whether in a strategy planning meeting, job interview or sales presentation. However, the key to the interrogation process is to never talk to anyone before the investigation is completed.

The system of monitoring verbal cues allows one to anticipate disbelief or cynicism, if the fingers touch the nose; concentration or interest, while stroking the chin; asking one to keep quiet, if fingers cover the mouth; and the appearance of confidence noted by steepling of the hands.[3]

Verbal Clues

Message	Appearance
Disbelief or cynicism	Fingers touching the nose
Concentration or interest	Stroking of chin
Shut-up, too much talk	Fingers covering the mouth
Confidence	Steepling of hands

Adapted from 3

The handshake is an often-studied part of the formal business interaction process. The "dominator" type handshake, marked by excessive force encourages the other participant to submit.[3] The "cooperator" mirroring the grasp of the partner suggests, "you are my equal." The "submissive" grasp indicated by an upwardly held palm says, "I'm here for you." The politician handshake indicates the "phony" double hand grasp indicating insincerity. Lastly, the "snobbish" approach is a dismissive weak grasp implying you are not significant enough for me to "even flex a muscle."

The Handshake

Type	Action	Message
Domination	Overpower	"Submission"
Cooperation	Equal	"You're my equal"
Submissive	Upward palm	"I'm here for you"
Politician	Two hands	"Insincerity"
Snobbish	Dismissive	"Don't even flex a muscle"

Adapted from 4

These observations have even been objectively studied in the business arena. Chaplin, in an article published in the *Journal of Personal and Social Psychology* tested the hypothesis that a firm handshake conveys a favorable first impression.[4] This study of 48 men and 64 women evaluated the strength, vigor, duration, completeness of grip and eye contact involved in the handshake. They found the handshake to be reliable predictor of personality and other behavioral traits, especially correlating in those who are more extroverted and expressive.

Clearly, both formal and informal programs that emphasize friendly positive encounters are viewed favorably in the business setting. In Japan, "flattery" both wins friend and influences people. Here, two young entrepreneurs—Yuzo Koyama and Keiya Mizuno offered a professional flattery service offered at $.95 per minute during the recent economic recession.[5]

Although, this concept potentially appears absurd to western culture, such blatant institutionalism of a commonly encountered American business practice is not so far from the truth. Traditionally, Japanese society has recognized *taikomochi*, a subtle art where a professional entertainer is hired to keep guests happy in a discrete fashion. In addition, *komegoroshi* utilizes excess praise to humiliate in a public fashion, "death by flattery" in other words.

This approach that utilizes quick wit, excellent thinking, a bit of irony and a ton of praise, when used informally in routine business interaction, allows both parties to be well served.

References

1. Johnson, James M. President Emergency Consultants, Inc., personnel communication, 1997.
2. Zimmel, Alisa A., District Sales Manager, Takeda Pharmaceutical Co., personnel communication, 1992.
3. Franklin, Stephanie. "Read my Bod: In the Business World Much of What's Said and Heard is Never Spoken." *Pittsburgh Post Gazette*, 11 March 2001.
4. Chaplin, W. F., J. B. Phillips, J. D. Brown, R. N. Clanton, J. L. Stom: Handshaking, Gender, Personality, and First Impressions. *Journal of Personal and Social Psychology*: July 2000;79(1):110-117
5. Magnier, Mark. "In Japan, Flattery Wins Funds and Influences People." *Los Angeles Times*, reprinted in the *Pittsburgh Post Gazette*, 4 Sept. 2000, C 1-2.

Chapter 5

Leadership

There are a multitude of models and ideas from those who profess to be leaders. Since 1776 no group, or specifically any military organization, has achieved such fame or success over such a prolonged period of time as the United States Marine Corps. Three qualities appear to stand out including first, extraordinary frontline leadership typified by General Lewis B. "Chesty" Puller (1898-1971) stating that "straight ahead is the shortest distance between two points."[1] Second, unparalleled *espirit de corps* is a crucial feature necessary for success, and is advanced by pride in the unit often encouraged by a leader who spends time with the troops, so to speak. Third, a tradition of battlefield aggressiveness encompasses the direct approach to obtaining goals and objectives. Incorporating those traditional principles with proven effectiveness can have beneficial effects on any business.

Reason for the Marines' Success
1. Extraordinary front line leadership
2. Unparalleled *esprit de corps*
3. Tradition of aggressiveness

Adapted from 1

It is often questioned why certain people are so successful. The Carnegie Institute in the 1930's performed a study addressing this issue finding that only 15% of the reason for success was attributed to technical expertise.[2] In most cases, 85% of success was due to skill in "human engineering," emphasizing the ability to get along with people and communicate effectively in the workplace.

Human Engineering
1. Get along with people
2. Communicate effectively

Adapted from 2

Recently, the U.S. Census Bureau of Hiring, Training, and Management performed a survey of 3000 employers asking about the most sought after skills found in a job candidate.[2] They described the most desirable attributes including a positive attitude and good communication skills. The bases of these skills are relevant schooling and solid training. This package includes previous work experience culminating in good professional references. They cite a positive attitude as a more important influence than technical competence in a particular area.

Top Six Most Sought After Skills
1. Good attitude
2. Good communication skills
3. Previous work experience
4. Good professional references
5. Solid training in the field
6. Sufficient relevant schooling

Adapted from 4

However, do not underestimate the importance of knowledge. A corollary to this concept is offered by a vignette illustrating a point concerning adequate knowledge and prior experience.

The story goes that the Federal Aviation Administration established a process to determine airplane windshield strength.[3] The process entailed firing a chicken carcass via a launcher that allows impact to occur at 500 mph to approximate that which could be encountered in a mid-air collision. Successful contact would potentially certify a safe windshield.

This process was transferred to the British Rail system, which desired to ascertain the strength of a new high-speed locomotive windshield. They found during their testing the airborne bird not only went through the windshield; but as well, through the engineer's chair and an instrument panel and embedded itself in the back of locomotive car's wall.

On inquiry as to what went wrong with the test, the process had been repeated correctly save for the omission of the *thawed* chicken, as the frozen variety was used instead.

A recent survey by Christian and Timbers of Cleveland, Ohio of 202 board of directors search panel members of over 150 companies found a list of qualities sought in a new CEO.[4] The most commonly desired attribute was integrity—found in 43%, followed by leadership—in 27%, experience—in 23% and intellectual capacity—in only 7%. Intelligence once again rates as one of the least important traits in the hierarchy. Honesty and the ability to direct personnel are paramount over communication skills cited in other comparisons.

The Top Four CEO Qualities

1. Integrity   43%
2. Leadership   28%
3. Experience   23%
4. Intellectual Capacity   7%

Adapted from 4

Although, there is extensive discussion of leadership skills and expertise, for many executives, early lessons often started closer to home. The internal voice that most commonly guides one's management style often comes from one's mother.[5] Jack Welch former CEO of General Electric, Company who grew up in Salem, Massachusetts described his stay-at-home mother as "uneducated, but smart" and his best friend enjoying all his activities. His memories include, first an attempt to always raise the bar to ensure ongoing success; and second, she would encourage him to perform better, but refrained from expressing disappointment if he faltered.

William Monroe, the CEO of Bertolli, North America learned this lesson from his mother who worked in a knitting factory raising five children by herself after his father's death, "Trust your instincts, when making decisions, don't second guess yourself."

David Blanson incorporates his "flawless execution" strategy into his business allowing 6700 Domino's Pizza Stores in 63 countries to reliably deliver over 1 million pizzas per day. His mother's careful approach is often invoked as motivation to ensure that "multiple employees flawlessly deliver a quality product and fast service to a wide array of customers." Growing up in Southeastern Michigan, Blanson's mother suggested that first, hard work is the most important component of whom you choose to be, and second, don't dictate, but attempt to instill personal confidence.

Mom's Influence on Success

1. Always raise the bar
2. Encourage performance without disappointment
3. Trust your instincts, don't second guess yourself
4. Hard work is the most important component to success
5. Don't dictate, instill personal confidence

Adapted from 5

Lastly, your mom keeps you humble, you are never a CEO to your mom.

Another approach to ensuring success as a leader is to use a scripting approach working backward from employee satisfaction impacting on management style. This process includes: First, offer regular feedback on work performance; Second, be friendly and helpful; Third, impart enough job knowledge for employees to make decisions about their work; Fourth, provide accurate information about important matters; Fifth, support employee suggestions that are meant to address existing company problems; Sixth, satisfy employee's need for communication concerning performance evaluation; Seventh, provide evaluation that is fair and objective; Eighth, offer an opportunity to participate in work environment decisions; and Ninth, encourage novel methods of job performance.[6]

Positive Supervisory Attributes

1. Feedback on work performance
2. Friendly and helpful
3. Job knowledge to make work decisions
4. Provide important information
5. Support employee constructive suggestions
6. Performance evaluation:
    a. Fair and objective
    b. Adequate communication

7. Participation in work environment decisions
8. Encourage novel work approaches

Adapted from 6

Leadership is often not a one-size-fits-all strategy—"being the right kind of leader at the right time is no easy task, but is absolutely necessary for enduring effectiveness," according to Guy Gage, a consultant with Toothman Rice.[7] The successful leader must possess traits in all five areas of leadership.

First, visionary leadership requires an awareness of the new and innovative, while rethinking the capacity to deliver themselves and by inspiring others. This capability requires the ability to both function optimally in the current environment, as well as develop innovative new pathways.

Second, achievement leadership becomes paramount when things are headed in the wrong direction, not when times are good. Their critical function includes obtaining results through intense focus-emphasizing outcome, and not process variables. However, the key to maintaining a moral entity is functioning within a proper value system.

Third, crisis leadership responds to externally imposed events, while change leadership deals with an internal nidus for new development. The net result, however, is the same. Stress and uncertainty have significant adverse impact on worker productivity and output. The key to this approach is maximum visibility, reassurance, and stability. Fourth, succession leadership is built on the premise of employee empowerment with management taking more interest in workers than their own success. This role is crucial. It provides support for the mentoring process to continue the supply of new leaders. Fifth, culture building leadership establishes a reliable practice of ideals and values that drive the operational aspects of the business. The most crucial aspect of this design is the manager's own conduct and adherence to pre-established value.

Lastly, millennial leadership dictates adherence to a rapid rate of change in today's marketplace. The successful leader requires more than a one to two attribute talent set and must be multi-talented and multi-faceted. In addition, they must be amenable to change, as the skill set may require quick transition to maintain marketability.

The Six Types of Leadership

		Tool	Attribute
1.	Visionary	Communication	Innovative
2.	Achievement	Focus	Outcome driven
3.	Crisis	Visibility	External factors
	Change		Internal factors
4.	Succession	Empowerment	Employee success
5.	Culture building	Purpose	Values
6.	Millennial	Versatility	Multi-talented

Therefore, it appears that the traits of leadership seem to reduce to a group of common attributes that include integrity, work ethic, the ability to communicate and work with others, as well as intellectual capacity.

References

1. Hoffman, Jon T. *Chesty: The Story of Lieutenant General Lewis B. Puller, USMC*. Random House, 2001, 1-696.
2. Kiyosaki, R. T. and S. L. Lechter. *Dad's Rich Kid, Smart Kid: Giving Your Child a Financial Headstart*. Warner Books, 2001, 1-264.
3. "The Airborne Chicken," Snickerz. Vol. 31/Issue 5, 16 Feb 2002, 9.
4. "What it Takes, Qualities Sought for a CEO by the Board." WSJ: In Christian and Timbers, Cleveland, Ohio, 2000.
5. Hymowitz, Carol. "In the Lead: For Many Executives, Leadership Lessons Started With Mom." *Wall Street Journal*. 2000.
6. "Evaluating the Boss," HR Solutions, Inc., 2001.
7. Gage, Guy. "The Five Applications of Leadership." *WV Executive*. Spring 2002, pages 23-27.

Chapter 6

Personnel Development

An integral aspect of business success is continued growth and personnel development, whether at an entry-level employee or the corporate CEO. From a management point of view, it is helpful to view issues through the eye of the employee, as to what factors appear to be the most important in job satisfaction.

An employee opinion survey offered by HR Solutions stresses meeting expectations of job satisfaction, career development, skill utilization, fair compensation, adequate benefits, good supervision, support from play suggestions, decision-making ability, consistency in policies, concern of senior management, job security, fair problem resolution, efforts not directed towards the area of no control and the ability to directly contribute as aspects of employment that improve satisfaction to further corporate goals.[1]

Desirable Job Attributes

1. Expectations are met concerning responsibility.
2. Employment as a career, and not a job.
3. Utilization of all skills and abilities.
4. For compensation.
5. Adequate benefits.
6. Employee suggestions are monitored.
7. Participate in work environment decisions.
8. Intradepartmental consistency.
9. Policies and procedures are followed.
10. Senior management has employee concern.

11. Adequate job security.
12. Management responds to problems fairly.
13. Job effort is directed towards things under control.
14. Direct employee contribution to success is possible.

Adapted from 1

Therefore, addressing these concerns has multiple benefits, where employees that are satisfied cause less administrative hassles, as well as ensuring superior performance utilizing a management assessment system based on employee satisfaction.

An additional mechanism to ensure maximum contribution of employee service is to institute a stable mission statement and set of operating guidelines that they can rely on.

The George W. Bush White House offers a general operating strategy through Andrew Card, Chief of Staff.[2] They suggest that first, business attire should be appropriate for the workplace—ties and jackets for men and proper business attire for women. Second, brevity in written materials is desirable. Ideally, briefing papers should be 1 to 2 pages long at most trying not to state the obvious. Third, punctuality is critically important. Staff should remember to try to be sensitive to the clock for both meeting start time and duration. Ideally, in fact, presenting a few minutes early for the meeting or staying a little later often shows extra interest and devotion. Fourth, respect is helpful in the workplace milieu with respectful treatment of co-workers or the requirement to return calls promptly.

Lastly, effective work habits include a work life balance avoiding a workaholic pathway, attempting to leave the office by 6:30 PM every day to spend time with the family or engage in some leisure activity. This approach offers a good balance between effective work place behavior and quality relaxation time.

Office Guidelines

1. <u>Attire</u>
   Appropriate business wear.
2. <u>Brevity</u>
   Don't state the obvious.
3. <u>Punctuality</u>
   First in, last out.

4. Respect
   Respect each other.
5. Work habits
   Don't be a workaholic.

Another helpful series of suggestions comes from Edwinia A. McConnell, who labored for 30 years as an R.N. in the healthcare work environment.[3] She offers these tips for staying on top; learning is a lifelong endeavor, know your worth, network extensively, express appreciation, give undivided attention to dialogue, self promote, negotiate terms in writing, wait to respond to request, acknowledge compliments—don't minimize your efforts, search the job market, don't engage an obvious combatant, know your control limits, monitor your attitude, track your successful behaviors, modify behavior for errors and be proud of your accomplishments.

The Way to the Top

1. Learning is a lifelong endeavor.
2. Know and promote your worth.
3. Network extensively.
4. Express appreciation in writing.
5. Undivided attention during interaction.
6. Advertise your accomplishments.
7. Written agreement in negotiations.
8. Respond to requests only after contemplation.
9. Don't minimize acknowledgment of your work.
10. Continue to monitor the job market.
11. Don't engage an obvious combatant.
12. Know your control limits.
13. Monitor your attitude.
14. Monitor performance-identify variables.
    a. Repeat successes.
    b. Correct failures.
15. Be proud of your accomplishments.

Adapted from 3

To build the most powerful company possible, the ability to answer these 12 questions from the employee perspective is crucial according to

Marcus Buckingham of the Gallup Organization.[4] Success becomes truly dependent on people's ability to vest in the enterprise.

Workplace Characteristics

1. Work expectations.
2. Material and equipment to perform the job properly.
3. Opportunity to do the best every day.
4. Receive recognition or praise.
5. Supervisors care about me as a person.
6. Encourage my development.
7. My opinions count.
8. Is my job important?
9. Co-workers committed to quality work.
10. Best friend at work.
11. Talked to me about progress.
12. Opportunities to work and grow.

Adapted from 4

References

1. HR Solutions, Inc., 2000.
2. "2002 White House Rules." Reprinted from *New York Times*. *Post Gazette*. 11 March 2001.
3. McConnell, E. A. "Getting Around-Fifteen Tips for Staying on Top." *Nursing 2000*. July 2000, page 69.
4. Buckingham, Marcus. "Twelve Questions That Matter." *Gallup Organization*. Princeton, NJ 1992-1999.

Chapter 7

Managerial Development

Once again, the key to managerial development begins with putting the right people in the right jobs. "No matter how inspiring a leader you are, you are only as effective as your team" according to Richard H. Brown, CEO of Electronic Data Systems of Perno, TX.[1] He also emphasized that being smart or proficient was not enough. "Being smart is the price of admission. What counts is how effective you are" as a leader.

Suggestions for an effective hiring strategy include finding those who first, try new approaches and compete fiercely to win customers; second, outperform peers noted by superior work history and habit of excellence; and are more energy suppliers, not energy drainers—finding a way to succeed at the task at hand.[1] The key to this process, however, is to blend both new and old talents to arrive at a balance between enthusiasm and experience.

The Right People for the Right Job

You should hire those who:
1. Are willing to try new approaches.
2. Compete fiercely to win customers.
3. Outperform peers.
   a. Good work history.
   b. Habit of excellence.
4. Blend old and new talents.
5. Choose energy suppliers—not drainers
      "I'll find a way"   "More shadow than sun."

Adapted from 1

Perhaps the most difficult aspect of managerial activity is the prospect of evaluating one's employees. The key to appraising others is to first, give honest feedback—a common pitfall is to give an above average review to avoid confrontation but this strategy should be limited as to protect morale of the other staff.[2] Second, ask questions—most employees won't volunteer information without some sort of prompting. Third, focus on the future, targeting upcoming goals as much as last year's performance. Fourth, communicate company goals as corporate priorities shift in a changing climate.

Appraising Others

1. Get honest feedback.
2. Ask questions.
3. Focus on the future.
4. Communicate company goals.

Adapted from 2

An effective technique for performance review is found at PPG Industries, a Pittsburgh based paint and glass manufacturer with 36,000 employees. They describe "SMART" goals that are definitive and concrete in that they are specific, measurable, agreed upon, realistic and time bound.[2]

"SMART" Performance Goals

1. Specific.
2. Measurable.
3. Agreed upon.
4. Realistic.
5. Time bound.

Adapted from 3

Lastly, the annual evaluation could be an opportunity for a positive interaction reaffirming the employee's efforts towards goal achievement.

Managerial development encompasses a wide variety of specialty skills and attributes. The "managing up" concept allows one to be effective in interactions with superiors.[3] The negative connotation of this attribute is to describe a boss more intent on impressing higher ups in helping support an employee's advance in the system. The positive connotation is to understand corporate goals, objectives, as well as supervisors' priorities in helping to direct staff to advance these goals.

Techniques to assist in development include first, not being afraid to speak up; second, to determine the new bosses preferred communication style; third, take advantage of informal meetings; fourth, networking with staff; and fifth, noting team accomplishments above individual accomplishments.

"Managing Up"

1. Don't be afraid to speak up.
2. Determine new bosses preferred communications style.
3. Take advantage of informal meetings.
4. Networking with staff.
5. Note team accomplishments.

Adapted from 3

A significant proportion of effort is directed toward development concerning job promotion. You should be sure to have the critical experience for the top job, where a washout is possible without adequate job skills. The key to success on the road to the top has been described by Edward A. Blechschmidt of Gentiva Health Services, Corbin A. McNeill, Jr. of Exelon Chicago Utility, and Frank Newman of Eckerd Company, the J. C. Penney Drug Store chain.[4]

The road to success in managerial progression includes first, the second in command needs access to all the key players; second, you should nurture strong relationships with the board; third, seek wide responsibility—attempting to research diverse areas currently not under their authority; fourth, learn the preferred corporate communication strategies; and fifth, transfer experience to new areas. Perhaps most importantly, after promotion one should prepare for isolation and develop an independent operating model since feedback sometimes becomes less once in a position of authority.

Road to Success

1. Second in command needs access to key players.
2. Nurture strong relationships with the board.
3. Seek wide responsibility—research diverse areas not under their authority.

4. Learn corporate communications.
5. Transfer experience to new areas.
6. Prepare for isolation and lack of feedback as the leader.

Adapted from 4

An important issue regarding corporate development is optimizing communication to keep informed in a global economy. First, you cannot plead ignorance and must understand all aspects of the business—"I don't know how you can make decisions and set policy if you don't know what is going on day-to-day" as stated by Edward J. Kelley, III; CEO of Mercantile Bankshares, Baltimore.[5]

Second, you should filter out what isn't critical and focus on the essentials. Rolf Stahel, CEO of Shire Pharmaceuticals, uses a traffic light system to delineate the important from less critical information utilizing a red, yellow and green light analogy for triage. Third, he also describes "management by walking around" striving for maximal employee face time. Fourth, you do not need to micromanage all the employees, and yet should be involved in all major decisions.

The key to this process is informal conversation—"If I don't contact them, they contact me," according to E. Kelley.[5] John Much, CEO of HNC Software, San Diego, CA, suggests that you should network from the highest to the lowest level employees, where his sessions are known as "java with John." This strategy allows one to serve as a moral compass reminding people of our own standards. Michael Bonsignore, the former CEO of Honeywell, spends at least 50% of the time visiting clients and customers stressing "straight talk with bad news." It is a daunting task to stay connected and focused in a global environment.

Keeping Informed

1. Cannot plead ignorance.
2. Filter out what isn't critical.
3. Focus on essentials.
4. Manage by "walking around."
5. Be involved in all major decisions.
6. Informal employee conversations.
7. Network from highest to lowest employee.
8. Spend half of your time with clients.

Adapted from 5

Lastly, the potential for a negative outcome must be considered. What if you are passed over for promotion—do you have a plan? The suggested strategy should address first, to ask why you didn't succeed and is change possible?[6] Second, are the improvements that you propose compatible with your ultimate career goals. Third, if you disagree with your supervisor ask colleagues for feedback and take that advice. Fourth, failure is an opportunity to develop new skills and talents. Finally, evaluate all aspects of your performance after losing a promotion.

Passed Over for Promotion

1. Ask why you didn't succeed. Is change possible?
2. Are changes compatible with your career goals?
3. If you disagree with superiors, ask colleagues for feedback and take their suggestions.
4. Is failure an opportunity for development?
5. Evaluate yourself after losing promotion.

Adapted from 6

From a managerial perspective, the most difficult scenario is the prospect of an actual job demotion. Lynn Morgan, the founder of Morgan, Walker and Associates, with $25,000,000 in revenue and sales in the year 2000, has experienced both ends of the employment spectrum—from owner to employee.[7] This experience recommends: first, don't be a "pain in the neck"; second, "be less pushy" as your authoritative role has been diminished; third, don't give too much information; fourth, adapt to a slower pace of change; and fifth, attempt to retain the good aspects of your former persona while jettisoning the bad which may have resulted in the demotion.

How to Survive a Demotion

1. Don't be a "pain in the neck."
2. "Be less pushy."
3. Don't give too much information.
4. Adapt to slower change in a large company.
5. Retain the good aspects of your old persona.
6. Keep your strengths.
    a. Evaluate objectively.
    b. Make logical decisions.

Adapted from 7

However, in the face of uncertainty and change; try to preserve your strengths and the ability to looks at things objectively, but always retain your core attributes that make you most desirable as a leader.

A significant difficulty exists with today's manager who has professional expertise and knowledge in productivity, but is lacking in the area of employee motivation.[8] Typically, rather than creating a helpful agenda providing support and allowing employees to flourish, they are often left to micromanage employee job responsibilities. This scenario can often occur when the employee is promoted to a position based on technical expertise and not leadership ability, as they are clearly different.

Several approaches have been offered to deal with this common dilemma. Lloyd Trotter, president of General Electric Industrial Systems, suggests a firm but gentle approach—being aggressive with weak managers to encourage departure, but working toward retention in stronger managers. This may take the form of offering an individually challenging position, directing away from the managerial role. Nina Smith, the chief marketing officer at Web Trends™ suggests the straightforward approach to dealing with a poor manager. She stresses confrontation when there is an employee detriment, with an instituted action plan handled privately with direct supervision. William Johnson, CEO of Heinz Company suggests the best remedy is to avoid the difficulty in the first place. Do not promote as a reward, substitute financial compensation for recognition, not a token manager's job.

An extremely common trait amongst the successful corporate CEO crowd is the so-called "boundless energy."[9] This trait is necessary in the global environment—moving through time zones, conversing around the clock, and using travel time to be productive. Personally, my most productive writing time has been during travel, allowing isolation and appropriate focus. Additional helpful strategies include minimizing caffeine intake, improving diet and a daily exercise program to blunt the rigors of today's business world.

Boundless Energy

1. Communicate through time zones.
2. Use travel time to be productive.
3. Maintain your health—manage stress

Adapted from 9

Most often, the best advice comes from experience, especially with job turnover or change. Hilary Stout relates the story of Kaleil Tuzman, former CEO of GOV Works™, citing funding failure in a turbulent market.[10] He was frank about mistakes made citing "the sins of premature entrepreneurialship." He suggests; first, if warranted, step aside early as CEO. Second, be sure to delegate effectively. Third, worrying too much about what people think about you results in poor decisions. Fourth, don't believe all the Internet hype to "go big or go home.." Fifth, don't hire all employees in your own mold. Encourage diverse skills to complement your own. Sixth, don't trust people who may not have a vested interest in success, potentially including venture capitalists, clients, employees and the media. You must know the motivation of each party. Seventh, spend your time wisely. Worry about "value creation" not just press opportunities.

"The Sins of Premature Entrepreneurialship"

1. Step aside early as CEO, if necessary.
2. Delegate more effectively.
3. Don't worry about what people think.
4. Don't believe the Internet hype.
5. Don't hire people too much like yourself.
6. Don't trust people who aren't motivated.
7. Spend time wisely—focus on value creation.

Adapted from 10

It is crucial to know when your job is in jeopardy so that adequate planning may take place for a transition. Joann S. Lublin offers her top 10 signs of troubled times, cited from layoff victims.[11]

First, be aware of changes in your boss's attitude that appear more forgiving such as approving a vacation, which may have already indicated a termination decision. Second, you lose key perks such as a privileged parking space. Third, gifts fall by the wayside. Dropping off the Christmas gift list is not a good sign. Fourth, subordinates invited to high-level meetings may be being groomed for a transition to your position. Fifth, although seemingly a positive, being asked to chair a corporate charity drive is a real red flag with employees never returning to their duties according to Robert Morgan, head of Spherion Consulting Group, the Fort Lauderdale staffing firm. Sixth, be aware of management double-speak-talks of new systems accompanied by time logs—inquiries of employee activities are often accompanied by job loss. Seventh, you should worry if your staff looks bored with nothing to do and no direction as workload shrinks. Eighth, likewise, breaking up your work team where employees are considered in the transition and the progress of your projects is requested. Ninth, the company hires and asks you to train people with skills similar to yours.

Lastly, co-workers may be uncomfortable knowing your proposed course either demonstrating overt avoidance or unusual friendliness and concern.

Top 10 Signs of Troubled Times Related to Continued Employment

1. Boss changes his attitude.
2. Lose key perks.
3. Omitted from gift list.
4. Subordinates invited to high-level meetings.
5. Asked to run the corporate charity drive.
6. Beware of management double-speak.
7. Staff looks bored.
8. Work team is broken up.
9. Asked to train new hires with skills similar to yours.
10. Peer relationships sour or sweeten.

Adapted from 11

Remember that loyalty on the part of employees must be truly earned and is often not necessarily delivered as a quid pro quo for the wage and salary. Richard Blow, author of *American Son, the Story of John F. Kennedy, Jr.,* stated this premise as "loyalty is owed in proportion to the character of the person to whom it is owed."[12]

References

1. Hymowitz, Carol. "In the Lead; Managers Tell You How to Spot Gold Talent in Old and New Hires." *Asian Wall Street Journal.* 27 March 2001, B 21.

2. Scherreik, Susan. "Your Performance Review—Make it Perform." *Business Week*. 17 December 2001, pages 139-140.
3. Hymowitz, Carol. "In the Lead; Being an Effective Boss Means Knowing How to Manage Up." *Wall Street Journal*. 22 February 2001.
4. Lublin, Joann. "Managing Your Career, You're a Good #2 But Are You ready to take the Top Spot?" *Wall Street Journal*. 6 February 2001.
5. Hymowitz, Carol. "In the Lead—How the CEO Can Keep Informed Even as Work Stretches Across the Globe." *Wall Street Journal*. 12 March 2002.
6. Frye, M. "Evaluate Yourself after Losing a Promotion." *Milwaukee Journal Sentinel*. October 1999.
7. Lublin, Joann. "Managing Your Career, How You Can Survive a Move to the Big Pond after Being the Big Fish." *Wall Street Journal*. 5 March 2002.
8. Hymowitz, Carol. "In the Lead; What Happens when Your Valued Employee Makes a Bad Manager?" *Wall Street Journal*. 23 January 2001.
9. Hymowitz, Carol. "In the Lead; How Some CEOs Get the Energy to Work Those Endless Days?" *Wall Street Journal*. 10 March 2001. D1.
10. Stout, Hilary. "Crunch Time; Chastened Tech Chief Aware of His Sins, Tries to Save Others." *Wall Street Journal*. 7 March 2001.
11. Lublin, Joann. "Managing Your Career; Left Out of a Meeting? Parking Space Taken? Worrying About Your Job." *Wall Street Journal*. 3 April 2001.
12. Blow, Richard. *American Son, John F. Kennedy, Jr*. Henry Holt, 2002, 1-294.

Chapter 8

Business Models

An extensive amount of discussion has taken place in the business arena where other endeavors and disciplines are analogized and extrapolated to use as a business model.

Military Model

An often-used experience, which has suggested adaptation to today's business world, is the military experience. A Navy Admiral with 49 years of service stated that when she cited the most significant change she found during her tenure, "We used to train and prepare leaders, now we prepare administrators."

These military models are adapted to provide an organizational structure or operating guidelines such as The Navy Seal teams, "Get it done" motto. "Top Gun Techniques" has been utilized to enable companies to learn from fighter pilots.[1] This "business is combat" model allows reservists to train corporate executives in a mock squadron bunker dealing with missile attacks, debriefing and strategy sessions costing up to $32,000 for 150 participants.

The squadron learns to respond as a team allowing one to first, react to contingencies; second, allow multi-task performance of duties; third, know your competitors inside and out; and fourth, assess your own strengths and weaknesses. This approach encourages the team concept with an interchangeability of personnel and dedication to the success of the mission.

Top Gun Techniques

1. React to contingencies.
2. Multi-tasking.
3. Know your competitors.
4. Strengths and weaknesses.

Adapted from 1

NASA Model

The NASA model is best typified by the "failure is not an option" admonition of Gene Kranz, the Apollo flight director. Gene joined the Mercury team in 1960 for ground up construction of a fight program including Alan Shepard's first in-space mission in 1961, John Glenn's thrice earth orbit in 1962 and the Apollo I tragedy. This approach was publicized in *Apollo 13*, the popular film portraying man's first lunar landing, as well as the harrowing one-in-a-million successful returns of the crew after mechanical failure.[2] This mission had a successful outcome based on an optimum combination of expertise, critical decision-making, and luck.

However, his modesty shines through with competence, discipline and morale; crediting others in the Apollo 13 "Tiger Team" success, including his wife, with the memorable mission vest idea.

NASA Model

1. Expertise.
2. Critical decision-making.
3. Good luck.

Adapted from 2

Sports

The professional and elite amateur sports model has been extended to operational areas as well. Some widely held corporate myths are clearly debunked by the self-evident truths generated in the sports world.

Myth #1: There is only the team and everyone contributes equally. Actually, most teams do have stars. On the 2001 New York Yankee Major League Baseball team there was a 63-fold differential between

Derrick Jeeter, who was paid $12.6 million and D'Angelo Jiminez, who was paid the league minimum of $200,000 as a shortstop.[3] Most corporate teams "suppress" rather than embrace this reality that some employees are simply more valuable than others.

Myth #2: Winners don't carry losers. In fact, the pay differential is significant in professional sports.[3] Another type of preferential treatment is the duration of the contract. In major league baseball, long-term contracts are only for superstars, while players with modest talent have contracts re-signed on an annual basis.

This issue also forced Jacques Nasser, former Ford Motor Company CEO, to a difficult position. He attempted to introduce a well-designed executive grading scale rated on an A-B-C basis, with 5% required in the latter category. He subsequently received an inordinate amount of criticism based on this "cruel, arbitrary, and heartless proposal." Likewise, Goodyear dropped a similar 10-80-10 employee grading plan under threat of litigation.

Myth #3: Trying hard is half the battle.[3] Actually, the 98th percentile is not good enough in competitive sports. In the Olympics, the time difference between gold and no medal at all is often less than 2%. During the 2002 winter Olympics, the time difference between winner and loser was 1.9% for the 10,000-meter speed skating event, 1.1% for women's giant slalom, and only 0.2% in the four-man bobsled. Therefore, being almost good enough—98-99% perfect, brought the participant nothing. Sports world insights such as these are invaluable in the analogy to business endeavors.

Sports Myths

1. Teams have stars.
2. Winners don't carry the losers.
3. 98th percentile is not good enough.

Adapted from 3

The NBA model has been offered by Phil Jackson, where he compares a professional basketball team to the typical Fortune 500 company.[4] This 7-time NBA champion, Zen influenced coach of the Chicago Bulls, on a daily basis attempts to motivate 12 "star players" to put aside personal differences to work as a team.

This group mentality dictates maximal productivity as guided by the coach, who helps to foster this approach by first, a sense of community providing motivation where all feel attached and valued; second, coach-driven teams are often losing teams, as opposed to those who are individually motivated; third, don't cater to star players alone—you must value the contribution of every person; fourth, acquire the benevolent dictator role as a means of leadership in a push, but only enough; and lastly, note that the team achieves a state of connectedness from pursuing a common goal.

Group Dictates Maximal Productivity

1. Sense of community provides motivation.
2. Coach-driven team is a loser.
3. Don't cater to star players.
4. Benevolent dictator model.
5. Connectedness from pursuing common goal.

Adapted from 4

The goal here is to realize that winning is the by-product of a plan to first eliminate an individual ego; second, accept their role in the team; and thirdly, to do what is best for the group.

Winning is a By-product of Team Mentality

1. Eliminate ego.
2. Accept role.
3. Do what is best for the group.

Adapted from 4

Medical Model

In 1986, Dr. Harry Gruber left a medical school teaching position to launch Gensia Biotechnology Research Firm then expanding to Viagene™, the nation's first gene therapy concern.[5] He found that there was a significant correlation between both the medicine and the business worlds. The analogies were first that listening to customers is like listening to patients, where 90% of the diagnosis in patients is made by history alone, minimizing the importance of the physical exam and even subsequent laboratory testing. Second, determining the patient or customer's needs is crucial to success. Third, listening skills either with patients or employees are critically linked to a proper diagnosis or plan, as well as significantly improved customer service. The patients are often less concerned about training or accuracy and more concerned about perceived treatment.

Proper Diagnosis for Business Success

1. Listening to customers is like listening to patients.
2. Determining customer needs allows a proper diagnosis.
3. Listening to employees is crucial to overall goals.

Adapted from 5

Information Technology

The interface of computer technology and customer service delivery is found in the Customer Relationship with Management model (CRM model)™, a novel operational approach to business implementation. The Seibel system experience with over 3,000 customers blends both personnel and processes to achieve organizational success.[6]

They suggest focusing on critical success factors that allow for successful implementation of this and other new information system technology. First, establish measurable business goals for without such "obvious factors, you will fail." Second, align your business and information technologies (IT operations), although it is still about the message and not the technology. Third, it is imperative that executive support be obtained prior to implementation of the new technology. Fourth, your business goals should pursue functionality as the main feature, if it doesn't directly impact the desired outcome and only serves process variables, it is often not necessary. Fifth, out-of-the-box functionality is significantly more efficient than that associated with excessive customization, resulting in unnecessary tinkering with the system.

Sixth, it is essential to use trained, experienced consultants expert in implementation, troubleshooting, and operations. Seventh, you should actively end-system users in solution design or you stand the risk of losing buy-in from those involved in implementation. Eighth, you should as well invest in training to empower end-users not just to generate the systems, but instead to achieve the valid business goals and objectives established by the organization. Ninth, ideally, you should use a phased rollout schedule. This allows establishment of a realistic series of steps and goals that allow success in a reasonable time frame.

Lastly, none of the successes matter without the ability to measure, monitor and track objectives. The key is to document what has been accomplished, as well as trying to achieve a continuous quality improvement (CQI) environment in the workplace.

Ten Critical Factors for Idea Implementation

1. Establish measurable business goals.
2. Align your business and IT operations.
3. Get executive support up-front.
4. Let business goals drive functionality.
5. Minimize customization—use out-of-the-box functionality.
6. Used trained, experienced consultants.
7. Actively involve end-users in solution design.
8. Invest and train to empower end-users.
9. Use a phased roll out schedule.
10. Measure, monitor and track your results.

Adapted from 6

In today's business parlance the "Five Nines" approach to business reliability, analogizing to 99.999% on line data availability in the computer model is often desired. It is crucial to realize, however, that the ideology and operational basics of the company is what is most important and the technology is the means and not the endpoint of the endeavor. Do not compromise employee motivation or initiative in the attempts to generate an absolute rigid, regimented efficiency process.

The Performance Model

Another approach is to take the presentation and performance model emphasizing public speaking skills on acting ability to business practice. Don Campbell suggests these tools to master the presentation process and possibly interface well with overall business performance.[7]

The key to the process is preparedness both to your message and then to the audience so that your presentation is precisely rehearsed and delivered. Second, starting promptly preserves the most precious business commodity—time itself. Delayed beginning often colors the remainder of the presentation.

Third, if you know your material well enough you do not need notes. There is nothing more disheartening than to have someone reading from a script and not interacting with the audience instead of making eye contact and asking questions or full participation with the audience relating their experiences.

Fourth, another cornerstone of the presentation is to be focused—establishing clearly defined goals and sticking to the plan. Pacing is especially important in that people have a limited attention span and are capable of assimilating information in 30 to 45 minute segments and recall drops off after that point—try to present factual information.

Fifth, the time is defined by knowing and defining your strongest points. Sticking with your plan as offered by Jim Endicott of Distinction Communication teaching presentation services to national and international companies. Likewise, both the opening and closing statements are crucial to establish the expectations, relevance, and credibility and to frame the context of the discussion.

Sixth, use the appropriate audiovisual adjuncts to get your point across. Often, using just enough material is better than too much, which is more commonplace in this age of the ease of electronic media. Some of the time a simple verbal rendition or graphic presentation is better than a multi-media barrage of data.

Seventh, a specific goal should be to encourage interest using a variety of techniques including humor; varying your delivery pace; and incorporating a range of activities—move around, challenge their interest or encourage two-way dialogue. Eighth, encourage and plan for participant interaction. In fact, you should try to incorporate interval exercise at regular periods during the presentation. However, it is important to keep the group continually moving forward and from being distracted from the goals at hand.

Lastly, the telltale sign of an inexperienced presenter is to run on too long. Please try to stay religiously within the allotted time frame whether it be 5 or 60 minutes.

Performance—How to Win over the Crowd

1. Be well prepared.
2. Start on time.
3. Be familiar enough to use only minimal notes.
4. Be focused with goals.

5. Stick to your plan.
6. Use audiovisuals to enhance, not substitute.
7. Encourage interest.
   a. Humor.
   b. Vary delivery pace.
   c. Range of activities.
8. Allow for participant interaction.
9. Keep the group on track.
10. End on time.

Adapted from 7

Although on the surface these recommendations often appear to be directed to the presentation process alone, it should be extrapolated to the entire business operations process of improving your discussion and secondarily your operational outcome.

Boxing

Teddy Atlas lived in the world of the boxer's code, "be inside or be outside, don't be halfway, make a commitment and stick with it."[8] Teddy, currently an ESPN II television consultant, progressed from a young, tough boxer under Gus D'Amato, who trained Floyd Patterson suggesting "will isn't as important as skill." Feeling fear is normal, just don't surrender to it, according to Teddy, a trainer of champions such as Mike Tyson and Michael Moorer.

His code has four simple rules to live by. First, never lie to yourself, face your weaknesses. Second, take responsibility for everything in your life and always push yourself to the next level. Third, live in the world of the absolute, not the relative. Fourth, there is no compromise. Sacrifice and obedience make a champion.

Making of a Champion

1. Never lie to yourself.
2. Take responsibility for everything.
3. Live in the world of the absolute.
4. Sacrifice and obedience make a champion.

Adapted from 8

Captain of the Ship

There is no operating model more dependent on a single individual than that of a sea boat captain. Dan Hupp, the vice president of Blattner-Brunner, an advertising firm, describes this observational experience with a fishing charter boat captain who offers this advice.[9] First, sell your business by promoting your crew and staff, specifically, promote the crew not yourself. Second, if you lose a crewmember replace them with someone better. Don't short staff and harm your clients. Third, communicate the love of your work to your clients and new prospects. Your work is your passion. Fourth, reveal your expertise and professionalism to your clients but don't damage their self-esteem. Fifth, perhaps most importantly, try to create your own raving fans. Hopefully, this no nonsense approach will deliver success, client support and additional referrals.

Captain of the Ship

1. Sell your business by promoting your crew.
2. Replace a lost crewmember with someone better.
3. Communicate the love of your work.
4. Reveal your expertise and professionalism without harming your client's self-esteem.
5. Create your own raving fans.

Thoroughbred Horse Racing

"Life is like the Kentucky Derby" as Dr. James M. Johnson, MD offers this life and business analogy vignette.[10] There are twelve of the finest racing horses brought to Kentucky Downs to hopefully win the Derby. The lessons are these. First, knowing the path is essential. Horses that race on some European tracks race in the opposite direction to American tracks, do not usually win the "Run for the Roses." Second, assembling a group of the "best of the best" has a previous first-time finisher moving to last place. Don't let this be disheartening enough to lose motivation. Most importantly, the first horse finishes clean and pristine, while the remainder of the field gets covered with mud. Those who have never had mud in their faces soon drop-off while those who have been through adversity can come from behind to win.

The "Run for the Roses"
1. Knowing the path is essential.
2. Even the best of the best can finish last.
3. Those that know adversity can triumph.

Factory Line Approach

Not to be outdone, near perfect results are pushed to the limit with the six-sigma approach.[11] The Greek letter "sigma" denotes a single degree of variation from the standard bell curve encompassing 69% of the population. Therefore, one sigma represents 690,000 defects per million events, three sigma—666,000 per million and six sigma—3.4 defects per million.

The goal is to reduce subjectivity in the process analysis and there are many variants to this strategy embracing the industrial approach. The first component is to define the process that is sub-par. Second, measure to determine current performance. Third, analyze the data to pinpoint where things can go wrong. Fourth, improve the process and eliminate the error. Lastly, put controls in place to prevent future errors.

Interestingly, this cost savings approach in error reduction has its basis in good sense normal job responsibility. We must legislate comprehensive and careful job performance today that came naturally to the previous generation of workers, your parents or grandparents. It is ironic that the information age required a reversal to a more basic production mode and ethic to be successful.

Factory Line Approach
1. Define.
2. Measure.
3. Analyze.
4. Improve.
5. Control.

Adapted from 11

In conclusion, the likelihood of success is improved by concentrating on the effective completion of one's own job, not worrying about "winning" alone.

References

1. Pascual, Aixa M. "Upfront, What Jet Jockeys Teach Desk Jockeys." *Business Week*. 11 March 2002, page 10.
2. Kranz, Gene. *Failure Is Not an Option, Mission Control From Mercury to Apollo 13 and Beyond*. Simon and Schuster 2000, pages 1-415.
3. Colvin, Jeffrey. "Value Driven, Think You Can Bobsled? Huh!" *Fortune Magazine*. 18 March 2002, page 50.
4. Jackson, Phil. "How to Motivate Your Employees." *Diversion*. 15 March 2002, page 66.
5. Sheehan, Michael. "Doctor Untangles the Web." *Physician's Money Digest*. 15 March 2002, page 35.
6. "Ten Critical Success Factors for Customer Relationship Management." Seibel Advertising, Fortune, 29 April 2002.
7. Campbell, Don. "Now Presenting, How to Win Over Any Crowd." *World Traveler*. April 2002, page 24.
8. Newfield, Jack. "That Makes a True Champion." *Parade Magazine*. 2 June 2002, page 8, 9.
9. Hupp, Dan. "The Private Sector; Oh, Captain, My Captain." *Pittsburgh Post Gazette*. 14 May 2002, B2.
10. Johnson, James M. The Greenbrier, Sulphur Springs, West Virginia Presentation. 19 April 2002.
11. Arndt, Michael. "Quality Isn't Just for Widgets." *Business Week*. 27 July 2002, p. 72-73.

Chapter 9

Success

If you were to choose the most successful businessperson of our time it would likely be Bill Gates, CEO of Microsoft, whose success is based on a simple decision to retain the rights to an operating system tied subsequently to all IBM personal computers.[1] After his years of experience including both successes and failures he settled on two areas that were most instructive to him. First, be careful about overconfidence. You will make mistakes so be prepared to change your course. Second, your most valuable commodity is your employees and your most valuable employees are those with a long-term commitment who are able to deal with the difficulties of day-to-day business dealings. Most importantly, unfair things will happen.

Business Success
1. Be careful about overconfidence.
2. You will make mistakes. Be prepared to change.
3. Your most valuable employees are those who:
   a. Make a long-term commitment.
   b. Deal with difficulties.
4. Unfair things will happen.

Adapted from 1

Examination for successful business models has run the gamut from conventional iron and coal hard industry to the ephemeral Internet information-processing realm with neither extreme being ideal. Stephen Hardis, CEO of Eaton Corporation, discusses lessons of both old and new economies.[2] This Lion of the old economy, founded in 1911 to make truck axles is still a major industrial manufacturer operating in 23 countries with 63,000 employees and $8.4 billion in sales.

Hardis suggests that you should first forget artificial distinctions between "old and new" technology and use novel techniques to improve untraditional profit making values. Second, the rules haven't changed. All successful companies are fueled by good ideas and ultimately profits matter. Third, the traditional values will still prevail. Industry survivors will manage growth, build infrastructure, and attract and retain new talent. Fourth, your customers will reflect your self worth as much as the stock market as the best estimate of your value.

Lastly, put your best foot forward attracting talent towards an undesirable market. If you live in the Snow Belt wait until spring to interview new employees. In conclusion, new technology should be used to improve solid conventional business foundation attributes found in the older business model.

Blending Old and New

1. Forget artificial distinctions.
2. The rules haven't changed.
3. Traditional values—Growth, infrastructure and talent will prevail.
4. Customers, not "the market," reflect your self worth.
5. Best foot forward to attract talent to an undesirable market.

Adapted from 2

John Chambers, who became a CEO of Cisco Systems with a market capitalization of 541 billion, the third most valuable company at its peak rising from $2 billion in sales and 3,000 employees to $20 billion in sales and 30,000 employees manufacturing computer networking equipment, suggests that maintaining focus is crucial.[3] He strived to maintain an operational model that first focuses on internal development. Second, targets effective acquisitions. Third, develops an ecosystem of interconnected partnerships. Lastly, favor a horizontal business model, not isolated vertical relationships. Clearly, the cornerstone of the system is strong, interlocked lateral competitor and customer relationships.

Maintaining Focus
1. Internal development.
2. Effective acquisitions.
3. System of partnerships.
4. Horizontal business model.

Adapted from 3

The Medical Group Management Association defined the performance and practices of successful medical groups, which are easily extrapolatable to the general business environment.[4] First, a clear philosophy of goals and objectives is desirable, where you define success in terms of what you are trying to accomplish. Second, attempt to achieve agreement amongst employees on philosophy and goals to ensure a customer-friendly culture. Third, plan to achieve success—"If you fail to plan, you plan to fail."

Fourth, try to enact defined measurable goals individualized to the enterprise. Fifth, the cornerstone of this program is the ongoing collection and review of data—"data is power." Sixth, the working model includes both quality products or services that must be accompanied by customer satisfaction—"Do not deliver one without the other." Seventh, the combination of both good personnel and excellent administrative leadership is essential. The most respected leader usually works out the best. Eighth, encourage employee involvement in operations. Use a committee structure to encourage participation in day-to-day activities. Ninth, communication and trust are imperative between the employees. Successful groups are "focused on productivity, communication and trust."

Tenth, knowledge of the market in which you are operating is essential. "Take into account the demographic structure and politics of the community." Eleventh, a commitment to hiring a good staff is helpful. "Better performers staff to higher levels." Lastly, investment in equipment and technology is important, but keep overhead costs in line with revenue. Overall success is dependent on adequate time, effort and planning put into the work process.

Performances and Practices of a Successful Group

1. Clear philosophy, goals and objectives.
2. Agreement amongst employees on philosophy and goals.
3. Plan to achieve success.
4. Enact definite measurable goals.
5. Ongoing collection and review of data.
6. Quality products and services must be accompanied by customer satisfaction.
7. Good personnel and administrative leadership.
8. Employee involvement in operations.
9. Communication and trust are imperative between employees.
10. Knowledge of market in which you are operating.
11. Commitment to hiring a good staff.
12. Investment in equipment and technology.

Adapted from 4

From an economic perspective, certain traits seem to be found in the more financially successful operations. Lewis J. Altfest, PhD, feels there are nine traits found in winning companies, which include: first, active stock acquisition by management; second, a positive earnings surprise, ideally better than predicted; third, again, the dominant market share; fourth, good public relations; fifth, have a handle on debt; sixth, obtain a higher return on equity; seventh, assemble a smart management team; eighth, strive for consistent and stable growth.[5] Lastly, it is ideal to be a leader, but as well it should be in a popular industry. There is only a modicum of success in being the best in a dying industry—analogous to the finest wagon wheel manufacturer. Certainly, it was a niche enterprise, but may not be relevant in today's marketplace.

Financial Traits of Winning Companies

1. Active stock acquisition by management.
2. Positive earnings surprise.
3. Dominant market share.
4. Good public relations.
5. Handle on debt.
6. High return on equity.
7. Smart management team.

8. Consistent growth.
9. Leader in a popular industry.

Adapted from 5

A significant stumbling block in today's business world is to operate in a restrictive manner emphasizing short-term objectives and goals. Steve Case, the CEO of AOL-Time Warner, Inc., emphasized that it is best to focus on the "far future" targeting long-term tangible goals.[6] The techniques best suited to managing from afar are, first, to hire terrific people and point them in the right direction while attempting to stay out of their way. Second, nobody can predict the future. You should stick to your vision and act. Third, set your operating plan 5 to 10 years in the future, don't get bogged down in day-to-day. Fourth, some forms of discussion are better than others—choose the face-to-face over telephone communication and voice mail over e-mail. Lastly, timing is everything, choose the time to seize the reigns again carefully.

Focus on the Far Future

1. Terrific people, right direction, no interference.
2. Nobody can predict the future.
3. Plan 5 to 10 years in the future.
4. Some forms of communication are better than others.
5. Timing is everything.

Adapted from 6

Therefore, your management plan is personnel based, forward thinking and emphasizing up-close communication and being sensitive to new opportunities.

An objective appraisal of success has been quantified as the American Customer Satisfaction Index, a survey of 200 companies and 30 government agencies sat on this rating scale. The University of Michigan Business School, American Society, compiles the rating scale for Quality and The CFI Group, graded 0 to 100 with 70 being the average value. They stressed the fact that you must manage expectations, as the consumer has become fickle and ever changing. Nordstrom's formerly was the highest rated retail chain in the survey, but the average score dropped steadily to 76. However, this still compares favorably to an industry average of 72.9, which decreased by 0.5% from 73.3 a year earlier.

Observations concerning this trend are offered by Claes Fornell, Professor and ACSI director, who suggested it is "squandering the benefit it once had." However, an alternative explanation is that the consumer's expectations may be too high for the service provided. Likewise, customer satisfaction grading scales can be poorly correlated with subsequent business success.

The 2001 ACSI customer service score found K-Mart to exhibit the largest retail jump—up 10.4% from a score of 67 to 74 while the company proceeded towards bankruptcy and reorganization.[8]

Eventually, the corporate officers encounter a situation forcing a struggle for survival. Analysis of these circumstances suggests that there are shared traits of leadership that are a common thread in the practice of successful CEOs.[9] First, it is essential to pacify angry customers fast, according to Jerry Levin, who took over Sunbeam Corp. in the setting of excess inventory, attempting to stoke short-term profits. This intervention was not enough, however, as the company eventually succumbed to market change. Second, stack your management team with former colleagues, or at least rally the troops to get to your side as offered by L. Dennis Kozlowski, who assumed control of Tyco International. He enlisted support with a promise to make the annual report more user-friendly to assist in the company transition.

Third, be frank with the board, but set expectations to a lower level. Gary DiCamillo, Polaroid Corporation suggests that you should never surprise the board, but also cautions that "candor never saves a consistent underperformer'.

Shared Traits of Leadership

1. Pacify angry customers fast.
2. Stack your management team with former colleagues.
3. Rally the troops to your side.
4. Be frank with the board, but set expectations to a reasonable level.

Adapted from 9

Eventually, the corporate officer encounters a situation where they are facing a struggle for survival. The transition of Wal-Mart stores began when founder Sam Walton transferred duties to David Glass in 1988, and then to H. Lee Scott in 2000 with prior planning predating this change by a 5-year preparation period.[10] This collective group offered advice to use this transition suggesting the prior CEO's careful planning and exposure to the board are essential to survival.

A comprehensive plan to deal with this transition includes first, the cross training of high- level executives in all business areas to avoid the steep learning curve found in transferring responsibility. Second, encourage interaction between the board and the new CEO to establish expectations for the new system. Third, rehearse the transition between old and new CEOs and watch for roadblocks by those obstructions to change. Fourth, it is wise for the new CEO to begin transition from the employee side of the table rather than in a dictatorial boss mode.

Transition to a Successful CEOs Succession

1. Cross train high-level executives in all business areas.
2. Encourage interaction between the board and the new CEO.
3. Rehearse transition between the old and new CEO.
4. New CEO should begin transition from the employee side of the table.
5. Stay humble.

Adapted from 10

Lastly, any change is perceived as less traumatic if you stay humble. Perhaps the best method of change involves a ground up analysis beginning from the customer perspective. A prudent approach is to attempt to anonymously traverse the trials of your customer service process to see things from their perspective, experiencing the process variables that may be cumbersome to your clients. This bare bones evaluation will expose some system weaknesses and strengths that can be addressed by an objective improvement process and continuous monitoring.

Likewise, the "growth at all costs" mentality may have plagued some portions of the Internet sales sector. Chris Zook of Bain and Company found in an analysis of the growth paths of 2,000 companies that only 1 in 10 have achieved true sustained profitable growth or a 5.5% average annual revenue growth over the past 10 years.[11] They defined the key to success to be maximizing one's core business, stressing three common pitfalls. First, failure to define the core business can be fatal. They found that 87% of the successful growth companies have a single dominant core business that can be expanded systematically, while only 3% have three strong cores or greater. However, it is crucial to change position if your core approach is obsolescence.

Second, failure to strengthen the core to its full potential before expanding aggressively may prove disastrous. The chance of success is less with the new product, while diverting resources away from the cornerstone product will weaken the company inherently. Third, failure to anticipate the challenges of movement away from the core can be described as overextension. Here again, limited resources are so diluted as to be ineffectual in all areas including the fringe area with success predicted at a 1 in 10 ratio. These recommendations with subtle adaptations to the particular industry should allow one to prevail in the ever-changing marketplace.

Your Core Business; Three Common Pitfalls

1. Failure to define the core business directly.
2. Failure to strengthen the core to its full potential before expanding aggressively.
3. Failure to anticipate the challenges of movements away from the core.

Adapted from 11

References

1. Wallrork-Winik, Lyrie. "You Have to Be Open To" *Parade Magazine*. 10 March 2002, pages 6 and 7.
2. Aeppel, Timothy and Claire Ansberry. "When Economies Converge." *Wall Street Journal*. 2000.
3. Thurm, Scott. "How to Drive an Express Train." *Wall Street Journal*. 1 June 2000, B1.
4. Jacob, Julie A. "Business Keys to a Successful Practice." *American Medical News*. 25 March 2002, pages 16-17.
5. Altfest, Lewis J. "Investment Consult, 9 Traits of Winning Companies." *Medical Economics*. 22 March 2002, pages 25-26.
6. Angwin, Julia and Martin Peers. "The Re-Emergence of Steve Case." *Wall Street Journal*. 17 January 2002, B1.
7. Bart, Patrick. "Economy, Winter of Discontent, Could Worsen that Slow Down." *Wall Street Journal*. 20 February 2001, A2.

8. Hilsenrath, John E. "Economy, Retailers Score Points in Keeping Consumers Happy." *Wall Street Journal*. 19 February 2002, A2.
9. Lublin, Joann S. "CEOs Guide to Survival." *Wall Street Journal*. 27 February 2001, B1.
10. Zimmerman, Ann. "How Wal-Mart Transfers Power." *Wall Street Journal*. 27 March 2001, B1.
11. Zook, Chris. "Manager's Journal; Amazon's Core Problem." *Wall Street Journal*. 2 April 2001.

Chapter 10

Competition

Rather than being a problem, competition should be viewed as an opportunity for improvements of processes or personnel. John Chambers of Cisco Corporation has seen both the rise and the fall of a computer network system development industry. He analogized operating in a competitive environment to driving an express train.[1]

First, you should make the customer the center of your work culture. This is best accomplished by directly tying compensation to customer satisfaction. Second, try to empower every employee to perform all tasks. The endpoint allows the employer to increase productivity and improve personnel retention. Third, you should create a corporate environment that thrives on change on both the managerial and worker levels. Fourth, optimum teamwork requires open two-way communication and trust.

Perhaps, the most important factor is the ability to build strong partnerships. This plan takes the form of active internal development planning for effective acquisitions and stressing partnership in a horizontal business model.

Managing Change, Driving the Express Train
1. Make the customer the center of your culture.
2. Empower every employee.
3. Thrive on change.
4. Teamwork requires open two-way communication and trust.
5. Build strong partnerships.

Adapted from 1

As the economy sours, you must make decisions and implement change at an even faster speed. Flexibility will help you weather a slumping economy.[2] Overall, your system should first monitor your business on a 24/7 schedule. Second, attempt to know your deepest values and goals and you will emerge better and stronger. Third, don't ignore the pain of expansion or contraction of the business concern, but be cognizant of incurring extra costs in the process. Fourth, stay visible and interact with your employees at every opportunity you can.

Weather a Slumping Economy

1. Monitor your business on a 24/7 schedule.
2. Know your deepest values and goals.
3. Don't ignore the pain of contraction of expansion.
4. Stay visible.
5. Seize opportunity.

Adapted from 2

Lastly, it is ideal to remain both aware and ready with enough preparedness to seize new opportunity as competitors rise and fall in the marketplace. Nortel Networks, a Canadian concern, attempted to transform an old economy culture to meet the demands of a new economy by refocusing on sale or acquisition. John Roth, CEO, offers right angle turn rules for staying competitive emphasizing "sudden refocusing."[3]

First, you should focus on leading edge new customers, not just old defensive "comfort customers." Second, time cannot be sacrificed for better quality, lower cost, or better decisions. Third, it doesn't really matter whether you develop or acquire the technology your business needs. Your role simply is to provide the technology that your customers require in a cost-effective manner. It is not important that you necessarily be the innovator. Fourth, when change becomes inevitable, try to lead and not just follow. Success is achieved by initiating change, not waiting for it to occur around you. Lastly, never be complacent and cannibalize products to maintain the edge for the short-term only.

Right Angle Turn Rules for Staying Competitive

1. Focus on leading edge, not just old stand-by-defensive customers.

2. Time cannot be sacrificed for better quality, lower cost or better decision-making.
3. It doesn't matter whether you develop or acquire your technology.
4. When change is inevitable, lead don't follow.
5. Never be complacent.

Adapted from 3

Sometimes the management responsibilities require moving in multiple directions simultaneously. Carly Fiorina, the new CEO of Hewlett Packard Company balances two separate distinct job arenas, both running the day-to-day operations, as well as waging corporate warfare, managing a response to proxy attempts at blocking the proposed acquisition of Compaq Company.

She suggests lessons learned on managing through distraction.[4] First, you should have both a strategic and peripheral vision to both look ahead and around issues that are encountered. Second, be proactive in communicating with employees about significant issues—ideally face-to-face over voice mail, which is preferred to e-mail. This particular point is oft cited and warrants emphasis. It suggests that personal communication is most desirable to encourage employee support during the threat of change. Third, attempt to be flexible. As the old saying goes, "stuff happens." Be both prepared and versatile. Fourth, build a strong team as success is derived from the right people and the concept of teamwork. Lastly, trust that you know more about your business than any other passive observer or critic.

Managing Through Distraction

1. Have both strategic and peripheral vision.
2. Be proactive in communicating with employees.
3. Be proactive in communicating with employees.
4. Be flexible.
5. Build a strong team.
6. Trust that you know more about your business than observers or critics.

Adapted from 4

Sometimes even with the best intentions "all hell breaks loose anyway" requiring you to minimize the effects of adverse public relations. Mitch Baranowski describes seven methods to minimize the damage and help to maximize the message.[5]

First, know your risks and, most importantly, assemble a crisis team proactively. Second, anticipate and plan for the worst-case scenario ideally stressing protocols and adverse scenario contingency plans. Third, form a crisis intervention team that drills regularly, at least annually. This is a surprise call or news conference.

Fourth, build your reputation bank, and then cultivate open lines of communication with the news media. Fifth, always tell the truth. You should always endeavor to communicate quickly, as public opinion is usually formed early, especially of the adverse nature. Sixth, try to do the right thing in every instance and you will not fail. Ideally, you need not explain why it has happened as much as how this or related events will not happen in the future. The key is honest explanation followed by a remedy for preventing future events.

Minimize the Effects of Bad Public Relations

1. Know your risks.
2. Plan for the worst.
3. Form a crisis intervention team.
4. Build your reputation bank.
5. Always tell the truth.
6. Do the right thing.
7. Incorporate what you learned.

Adapted from 5

Lastly, incorporate what you learned from the adverse experiences you weathered. The overall strategy should be to endeavor to learn from experience, debrief the staff, refine your operational plan to deal with this dilemma in the future and strive to prevent future occurrences in a proactive fashion.

Response to Adverse Experience

1. Learn from mistakes.
2. Debrief the staff.
3. Refine your operational plan.
4. Prevent future occurrences.

Adapted from 5

References

1. Thurm, Scott. "How to Drive an Express Train." June 1, 2001. B1
2. Hymowitz, Carol. "In the Lead; Speed and Flexibility Will Help You Weather a Slumping Economy." *Wall Street Journal*. 9 January 2001.
3. Heinzl, Mark. "Buying Into the New Economy." *Wall Street Journal*. 2000. B1, 4.
4. Tam, Pui-Wing. "The Chief Does Double Duty." *Wall Street Journal*. 7 February 2002. B1
5. Baronowski, Mitch. "When All Hell Breaks Loose." *American Way*. 1 February 2001, pages 94-96.

Chapter 11

Crisis Management

The culmination of planning and preparation strategy often results in testing of your operational approach to deal with a potential problem. The recent experience with Firestone Tire, a company under siege, illustrates the trials and tribulations encountered while trying to restore the public trust by using a professional crisis manager.[1] They generated a plan involving things to do or perhaps more importantly, not do, to accomplish this endpoint.

Positive interventions include: first, speed is crucial to the process. Rich Blewitt, president of Rowan and Blewitt suggests, "if you don't currently have an answer to the problem, you had better be able to relate to your group that you are working on one." Second, place your customer's interest above your own. "The company must seem to attempt to come to the aide of the people in crisis first and serve their own corporate interests last," according to Larry Kamer, managing director of the GCI Group. Third, always take a long-term view—as evidenced by the McNeil Pharmaceutical Company Tylenol ™ recall, where short-term sacrifice will salvage the corporate reputation in the long-term.

Strategies to avoid include, first, hide what you know. If you are only one step behind the wrongdoing evidence trail, not only is credibility damaged, but as well is the ability to control the spin, according to Victor Kamber, CEO of the Kamber Group. Second, get tied down in the day-to-day running of the company operations. If an event occurs, make the crisis the number 1 priority "you have got to drop everything and mobilize your folks to selectively deal with the problem in a focused way." Third, forget that public perception is more important than reality. "All that matters is what the customers think is reality, not what the actual facts or circumstances are," according to Stephen Fink, president of Lexicon Communications Group.

Restoring the Public Trust

Things to Do:
1. Recognize that speed is crucial.
2. Place customer's interests above your own.
3. Take a long-term view.

Things you should Not Do:
1. Hide what you know.
2. Get tied down in the day-to-day operations of the company.
3. Forget the fact that public perception is more important than reality.

Adapted from 1

The secret of restoring the public trust appears to be staying ahead of the adverse information, dissemination of positive information and being honest and truthful in your revelations while working to prevent future occurrences.

The experience of Microsoft CEO, Steve Balmer has been utilized to formulate a plan for managing a company under siege.[2] He began by directly jumping into the "hot seat" by assuming CEO duties in January of 2000. His suggestions are, first, begin with an attempt to narrow and simplify goals. Second, continue improving your product and services. Third, know who your key employees are and dedicate yourself to optimizing their state of well-being. Fourth, keep all employees informed of significant changes and pay attention to their concerns. Fifth, take to the road and see your customers on a frequent basis. Lastly, keep the customers apprised of proceedings and developments as time goes on.

Managing a Company Under Siege

1. Narrow and simplify goals.
2. Continue improving products and services.
3. Know your key employees and dedicate yourself to their well-being.

4. Keep all of your employees informed and pay attention to their concerns.
   5. Take to the road and see your customers.
   6. Keep customers apprised of new developments.

Adapted from 2

An integral part of the crisis management strategy is learning to prosper from a corporate makeover. Leslie Wexner, who founded The Limited™, in 1963, opened the first store in an Ohio shopping center and by the 1980's had thousands of stores.[3] However, by 1993, the company ran out of steam compared to nimbler more versatile competitors such as The Gap™ and Abercrombie and Fitch™. Interestingly, however, even the latter retailers went through the own hard times, as retail consumers can often be fickle, subsequently taking their business elsewhere.

His recommendations for the corporate makeover process include first, to accept the fact that change is good. Second, do not try to reinvent the wheel. Repeat what has worked before successfully. Third, the most important asset of every organization is its people. You should both choose your employees carefully, and then take care of them. Fourth, quickly point out flaws and reward successes. Lastly, set priorities because you can't do everything, so establish a hierarchy.

Surviving a Corporate Makeover

   1. Change is good.
   2. Don't try to reinvent the wheel.
   3. People are the most important asset of any organization.
   4. Quickly point out flaws.
   5. Reward successes.
   6. Set priorities.

Adapted from 3

Nordstrom's was another retailer who ran into difficulties with changing consumer sentiment.[4] They have gone through a gut wrenching effort to transform an older retailer to a more modern age trading tweed blazers for leather miniskirts. This family-owned and run retailer was an early true innovator of a positive customer service interface. The prototype customer service program suggested that *every* employee was empowered to help with *every* problem. This concept was truly revolutionary where the doorman or janitor could intercede on a customer's behalf to address problems and concerns earlier rather than later, when they are still remediable. The next crucial component of this system is to give all employees direct access to top management to remedy customer concerns.

Emerging From a Pile of Problems

1. Empower all employees to help.
2. Give all employees access to top management.
3. Continually reinvent yourself.
4. Don't lose your loyalist base to win new customers.

Adapted from 4

Remember, as you try to reinvent yourself for a younger market, realize that loyalists are put off by change, so don't lose your consumer base in an attempt to attract new customers.

When you face problems on every level and at every turn, whom do you trust—no one? Linda Wachner, CEO of Warnaco Group, a clothing manufacturer selling garments under lines such as Ralph Lauren, Speedo, Olga and Calvin Klein, offered advice on steering through a squall based on their past litigation experience.[5]

Miss Wachner offered these suggestions for leadership during troubled times. First, try to focus on what is important and do not be distracted. Concentrate on a single solid project and avoid jumping around to achieve the best results. Second, deliver the product or service the customer desires but grow along side them. It is crucial to remember that things change inevitably, and monitor trends to deliver the product of tomorrow not just today.

Third, trust your instincts and when push comes to shove, rely on yourself first. However, you must be confident that the right path has been chosen based on your own morals and integrity. Fourth, when choosing personnel it is important to respect their intellect and good judgment, as well as choosing only those whom you trust.

Lastly, the business community, although vast, is yet relatively a small, closed environment in some respects, so choose whatever colloquialism you prefer—"what goes around comes around" or the old adage—"do unto others" but be prepared to interact with others honestly in this environment to save yourself grief down the road from acquiring an unsavory reputation.

Leading In Troubled Times

1. Focus—don't get distracted.
2. Give customers what they want.
3. Trust your instincts.
4. Rely on yourself.
5. Choose people whom you respect.
6. "What goes around comes around," so "do unto others."

Adapted from 5

Finally, some things are just self-evident in this modern business world—as true today as always. The experience of Robert Steed Miller and his "tell it like it is style" as a turnaround specialist has proven value in today's business environment. He has been referenced in business clean-up operations that have included concerns such as Federal-Mogul Corporation, an auto parts supplier; Waste Management, Inc. in 1996; and the Chrysler buyout in 1980.[6]

During a difficult turnaround process, this "no nonsense" rhetoric suggests that first and most importantly tell everyone the truth. Interestingly, my interest in business analysis was born from a statement from a medical school associate dean in 1996 who stated, "lying is okay, in today's business world as an acceptable method of achieving a desired endpoint."

Although I was initially aghast at such a statement, subsequent political and corporate developments at the dawn of the new millennium proved him to be a visionary in his revelation. Next, you should make proper decisions, but don't study things to death. A simple good sense assessment is usually enough and further delay is often detrimental. Most things that need to be done are plainly obvious to most involved, so keep moving forward.

No Nonsense Talk

1. Tell everyone the truth.
2. Make decisions.
3. Research but don't study things to death.
4. Most things that need to be done are plainly obvious.
5. Listen to the customer.

Adapted from 6

Most importantly, listen to your customers. Their perspectives on your business operations are invaluable.

References

1. Kranhold, Katheryn and Erin White. "The Perils and the Potential Rewards of Crisis Managing for Firestone." *Wall Street Journal*, 7 September 2000. B1
2. Buckman, Rebecca. "Keeping On Course in a Crisis." *Wall Street Journal*, 8 June 2000. B1
3. Quick, Rebecca. "The Makeover That Began at the Top." *Wall Street Journal*, 25 May 2000. B1
4. Spurgeon, Devon. "In Return to Power the Nordstrom Family Finds a Pile of Problems." *Wall Street Journal*, 2000.
5. Quick, Rebecca. "Steering Through a Squall." *Wall Street Journal*, 10 January 2001. B1, 4.
6. Lublin, Joann S. "Tips from a Turnaround Specialist." *Asian Wall Street Journal*, 3 January 2001. B1, 3.

Chapter 12

Employee Stressors

Perhaps the best way to ensure a successful business enterprise is to attempt to see things through the eyes of your employees. For a single point of clarity it is helpful to remember that over 77% of Americans could not afford to write a $500.00 check out of their monthly budget without being overdrawn, citing the Levin Group.[1] Secondly, there are over 100 million people, or 40% of the U.S. population, in the workforce with median weekly earnings of $576.00, approximately $1,900 a month and $22,000 annually.[2]

Further analysis of the median employee weekly income finds approximately a 5-fold difference between the highest and lowest weekly wages reported by the Bureau of Labor Statistics.[3] But there may be a 40-fold difference between the CEO and the employee. The highest weekly wage earner was a physician. taking home $1,340 per week followed closely by lawyers earning $1,304 a week and finally a cashier who makes $285 a week.

Median Weekly Income (Dollars)

Professional	Trade	Entry Level
Physicians $1,340	Police $908	Dental Assistant $414
Lawyer $1,304	Firefighter $802	Hairdresser $343
Pilot $1,283	Teacher $782	Cashier $285
Pharmacist $1,243	Clergy $750	
Marketing Manager $1,074	Carpenter $533	

Adapted from 2, 3

The most recent analysis of job desirability comes from the "Jobs Related Almanac" noting the best overall job to be a biologist, earning $92,000 annually with great future job prospects, with the worst ranking 250th for a lumberjack.[4]

The best working environment was, as well, in the service field with the statistician ranking highest. Interestingly, the president of the United States or a firefighter ranked the worst. From a financial perspective, the salary range extends from $16,046 as a dishwasher to $4,637,825 annually playing for the National Basketball Association. Lastly, the stress component is least as a musical instrument repair person, with, once again, the U.S. president or a firefighter figuring most prominently in the stress arena. The beauty of the situation is that if there were one perfect job everybody would want it. Secondly, there is someone for every job.

Best and Worst Jobs

	Best	**Worst**
Overall	Biologist	Lumberjack
Working Environment	Statistician	U.S. president
Salary	NBA Player ($4,637,925)	Dishwasher ($16,046)
Stress	Musical Instrument Repair Person	U.S. president

Adapted from 4

Workplace stress results not just from decreased compensation but perhaps even more feared is the prospect of impending job loss. A survey of 2,900 laid off clients by Drake, Beam & Morin, an outplacement service suggests that the average job tenure has decreased yearly,[5] decreasingly most recently from 9 years average to 7 years average in the workplace at that particular job.

Average Job Tenure

Year	Tenure (years)
1999	9
2000	8
2001	7

Adapted from 5

Financial inequity manifests itself as significant employee dissatisfaction, wanting to give the boss a "pink slip." This propensity to want to fire the boss is inversely proportionate to salary, as reported in a telephone survey of 1,002 adult employees by Maritz Research.[6] They found that the desire was highest (28%) in those who made $25,000 or less annually, dropping to half that (12%) in those who made $75,000-$100,000 per year as an annual salary. There was, however, a slight bimodal peak increasing to 17% of those who make over $100,000 a year, an interesting finding.

"Pink Slip" for the Boss—Desire to Fire the Boss

Salary (dollars)	Desire (percentage)
Less than $25,000	27.5
$25,000-$55,000	22.5
$55,000-$75,000	13
$75,000-$100,000	12
greater than $100,000	17

Adapted from 6

Obviously, at the managerial level it would behoove you to consider this compensation discrepancy issue when trying to influence performance, with encouragement working better than offering only negative feedback.

Particularly, the business merger and acquisition process often triggers both an increase in worker anxiety and lower staff morale. Not only do employees fear subsequent job loss, but as well, experience the frustration of working for total strangers in a new operational setting and units, according to Joann S. Lublin's analysis.[7]

The total value of worldwide acquisitions in the merger process has increased by 5.1% to $3.5 trillion with 37,000 deals being contemplated annually. Interestingly, the majority (75%) fail to meet pre-stated financial goals and objectives in the merger with a direct adverse impact on the bottom line, according to Thompson Financial Securities data.

The story of David R. Brown adds a personal note to the discussion of the president/CEO of Stackteck Systems, Inc., a Toronto based producer of plastic injection molds to make containers. The company became a target of multiple takeover attempts and he had begun to lose sleep, skipped lunches and toiled longer to impress his new bosses, and at one point worried about having a heart attack.

Workplace consultants such as Mitchell Mark, suggest that employees frequently exhibit the vegetative signs of depression—losing sleep, gaining weight, resuming smoking or increasing alcohol consumption with stress levels directly proportional to their position within the company. In fact, the reason for leaving a newly merged company is stress "over 50% of the time," according to Robert Morgan, president of Spherion Consulting Group.

The Adverse Effects of Stress

1. Depression.
2. Smoking resumption.
3. Decreased sleep.
4. Weight gain.
5. Alcohol excess.

Adapted from 7

In this day and age the combination of increased job demand, longer hours, less compensation, and job uncertainty can manifest as "desk rage" resulting in verbal and physical outbursts, according to Daniel Costello's analysis.[8] Lost tempers are very common, raising the issue of workplace violence. A survey on workplace stress released in 2000 by Marlin Company of North Haven, Connecticut found that 42% of respondents suggested that yelling and verbal abuse happen frequently in their workplace.

An expert group of workplace psychology consultants including Mitchell Messer, Director of the Anger Institute, in Chicago and R. Brayton Bowen, the president of the Howland Group, suggest that these are warning signs of a colleague approaching a breaking point. The possible indicators include; first, skipping group lunches, a clear sign of demoralization as one loses interest in the work community.

Second, coming to work late is one of the earliest markers as motivation decreases. Third, the practice of calling-in-sick, as a self-help remedy increases when employees feel they can't get a break at work. Fourth, withdrawing from the customary office banter or social functions can be an unhealthy form of distancing oneself.

Perhaps, the most subtle maneuver is the activity of obsessing, where inappropriate focus is directed towards insignificant matters or an inordinate amount of time is spent on minute details.

This pattern usually means anger or frustration has overwhelmed their ability to appreciate the big picture with the appropriate hierarchy of significance.

Warning Signs of Workplace Stress

1. Skipping group lunches.
2. Coming into work late.
3. Calling-in-sick frequently.
4. Withdrawal.
5. Obsessing over small details.

Adapted from 8

Some companies have appreciated this point and delineated both unacceptable and acceptable ways of dealing with a stressful situation, such as, by sneaking a break.[9] Unacceptable actions include: first, self-evident conspicuous loafing behavior such as sleeping, playing computer games or Internet shopping which are obviously prohibited. Second, it is inappropriate to bring personal issues to the workplace, such as family or business disputes, divorce matters, billing or collection issues, etc. Third, refrain from behavior that is offensive to colleagues by surfing Internet pornography sites or other inflammatory political opinion Internet areas.

Lastly, do not openly seek other employment opportunities from the workplace. These behaviors are counterproductive to the work setting and disrupt the milieu of coworkers. On the other hand, these are behaviors that may be productive if mutually agreed upon by workers and management. First, it may be helpful to take breaks at relaxing times—early in the day, at lunch time, and late in the day—so that work efficiency is not disrupted.

Second, you should try to perform some personal errands during the workday that you may not be able to perform after hours. The quid pro quo is that a few minutes spent during the "business day" may save hours of time and frustration at home, allowing personal recharging and improving workplace efficiency—allowing you to even perform some work tasks at home, benefiting the employer as well.

Third, it is acceptable and often helpful to improve worker cohesion by allowing employees to converse amongst themselves or with friends and family at home. Lastly, the ability to leave a stressful workplace and increase one's physical activity is perhaps the most helpful intervention of all.

Workplace Stress Avoidance Behavior

Unacceptable	**Acceptable**
1. Conspicuous loafing.	1. Break at appropriate times—early, lunch and at 4:30 PM.
2. Sleeping.	2. Run a productive errand, for example: pick up a prescription.
3. Computer games.	3. Chat briefly with friends or family.
4. Open arguments.	4. Exercise—go to the gym, take a walk.
5. Home disagreements.	
6. Offensive web sites.	
7. Open new job search.	

Adapted from 9

Certainly, life has gotten more difficult for people and this is manifested as an increase in rudeness encountered in daily activity affecting both sides of the sale process. This development is reported from a study of 2,000 people by a nonprofit group, Public Agenda, for the Pew Charitable Trust.[10] They characterized the "land of the rude," where the random survey reported a wave of adversarial interactions including discourtesy, profanity, and lack of consideration. They attributed this change to a failure to teach children proper manners while television provides poor role models.

The business world finds that over 57% of customers with annual incomes over $75,000 have walked out of stores with only perceived positive perception of improved public behavior towards the elderly, disabled or minorities.

Dr. Borhl Wadsworth, the president of Public Agenda, suggests that it is a "daily assault of selfish behavior on the highways, in the office and in the stores" and attributes this rise in rudeness to home and work overload in people's lives. An interesting twist is—although 90% of the survey participants suggest that rude employees should be referred to management they acknowledge that the employee often gets no respect and is often the target of verbal abuse as well. Overall, this appears to be a national problem with 79% of respondents noting a "lack of respect and good manners."

The proper workplace has a level playing field with the same rules for customers and employees—no matter who they are. As often as not, in an aggressive business environment, the customer is at fault primarily with unreasonable demands or objections, as much as the employee is.

A fairly common theme in employee frustration is the likelihood of laboring on unfulfilling or unrewarding tasks.[11] First, the trend extends to middle management as well with the greatest discontent emanating not from hard work or long hours but from impossible expectations. Clearly, this is a no-win scenario as the bar continually rises. It is best to establish reasonable objectives that can be achieved by most employees and then modify behavior that is not achieving the standard. Second, another area of concern according to Gerald Kraines, president of Levinson Institute of Cambridge, Massachusetts, is that most managers today are well intending to provide and ensure customer satisfaction but are not empowered to achieve these goals. They are asked to solve significant problems and work dilemmas without proper tools, resources, or the authority to make changes or discipline employees. Third, "a mistaken identity syndrome" occurs to middle managers when they are promoted to a level of activity at which they are uncomfortable with themselves or disliked. This is a modification of the Peter Principle where the employee rises to a level of incompetence with a poor match between talent and task. Ultimately, the process leaves them frustrated, unable to extract themselves from a mundane workplace with tasks spilling over to their private life as well.

Is It the Work or the Expectations?

1. Impossible expectations.
2. Solve problems without resources.
3. "Mistaken identity syndrome."
4. Unable to extract themselves.

Adapted from 11

The logical next question is, can things get any worse? The answer is most certainly "yes," when you add financial uncertainty to a general level of job overload. If anyone is asked today about his or her stress level, it is stated that it is very high. "Oh, I have *so* much stress in my life." Interestingly, even in this complex world, today's stress pales in comparison to the stressors encountered by your ancestors.

"Stress was a hardy perennial in the textile mills and meat packing yards of the 19th century and the factories and the offices of the 20th century," according to Nancy Koehn, the business historian of the Harvard Business School.[12] She cites complaints in letters from a wide range of individuals from business tycoons to commodity clerks that state "no one has the time to stop and give a stranger directions or time for family or community service." Of note, these comments are not contemporaneous, but discuss events occurring at the turn of the 20th century, not now.

A study of 1,200 Pitney Bowes employees ranging from receptionist to executive managers notes having to deal with an average of 204 messages a day including e-mail, voice mail, regular mail or memorandums, as offered by Paul Finkle, CEO of HRPath.com, an online human resource company based in Alameda, CA.

This situation results in; first, a loss of control with too much information, from too many different sources. Second, these augmented communication resources result in a 30% increase in workload without any additional compensation. Second, this ready access of electronic communications destroys one's home privacy as well as producing information overload. Third, some occupations actually thrive on stress, such as paramedics, the law or military. Lastly, changes are more easily tolerated if compensation is increased appropriately.

Workplace Stress

1. Loss of control.
2. Information overload.
3. Ready access destroys home privacy due to electronic media.
4. Workload increase.
5. Some thrive on stress.
6. Tolerability is proportional to compensation.

Adapted from 12

However, the presence of workplace stress is felt more acutely in down economic times with a 53% decrease in stress relating to claims in boom times (1998) compared to down economic times (1993). Even in 1998, the median job absence for stress-related conditions was 15 days annually in 1998, according to the Bureau of Labor Statistics.[13] Although, initially, cost cutting and efficiency maneuvers may positively effect the bottom line, after some time these changes may be counterproductive as morale decreases due to the effects of negative stress.

Ideally, there should be a balance between the so-called "good—productive stress" and the "bad—counterproductive" variety. Clearly, job stress is rising from a 1999 survey of 2,500 workers with the proportion of employees acknowledging worsened stress to increase from 31-33% from the year previous, according to the Yankelovich Monitor.[14]

Similarly, the two extremes of stress have been identified and studied, comparing the effects of stress on work outcome. This work evaluated 2,000 managers and 450 lower ranking workers and was performed by Wendy Boswell, a management professor from Texas A&M and John Boudreau from Cornell Center for Advanced Human Resource Studies.

They generated a "good—challenge stress and bad—hindrance stress model." The challenge stress model emphasizes a productive outcome. First, job responsibilities should include multiple projects, assignments and responsibilities increasing versatility; as opposed to specialization to the point of boredom.

Second, employee's evaluations should be merit based, referencing the value to the organization; targeting salary, skills, or promotions rather than being popularity based. Third, those who are satisfied in the workplace tend to be loyal, and not looking for new work saves retraining costs for "revolving door" employees.

The hindrance stress model illustrates a poor performance outcome based upon wasted energy directed away from corporate goals and objectives. Factors that should be avoided in the business model include, first, try to eliminate the "red tape" or extensive administrative process that can be responsible for goal confusion. Second, there is nothing that more quickly results in a stalled career by disrupting employee motivation, than to have politics rather than performance shape employer decisions. This results in significant employee dissatisfaction, resulting in an ongoing job search.

The Good Stress, Bad Stress Model

Challenge	**Hindrance**
Good	Bad
Multitasking of projects and assignments	Goal confusion and red tape
Employee merit based evaluation	Political advancement
Happy	Dissatisfied job hunting
Loyal	

Adapted from 14

An adaptive strategy to cope with job loss experience has been offered by Jeffrey Zaslo of *The Wall Street Journal,* summarizing reader's experiences.[15] Advice for out-of-work readers for their colleagues include first, force yourself to be outgoing. Networking often requires you being in uncomfortable situations to be successful. Second, expect to be lonely. It is your personal search and responsibility. Third, work on your game face, be an actor. Lastly, be upfront and positive to be successful in your new endeavor.

Advice for Out-of-Work Colleagues

1. Force yourself to be outgoing.
2. Expect to be lonely.
3. Work on your game face.
4. Be upbeat.

Adapted from 15

Perhaps, the most crucial aspect of a job loss scenario is the family or friend interaction, which can be positive or negative. These recommendations may help. First, touch them. Kathleen Dixon Donnely relates the story of a friend's advice after being laid off as an assistant professor at Florida International University. "Being laid off is nature's way of telling you that you were in the wrong job." Second, make a loving gesture. It goes a long way. Third, quit asking about prospects. Ask how you can help. Fourth, remember it is not about you. They don't want to hear your job loss story. Fifth, read the newspaper. There is often information on who is hiring and who is not. Think before you speak. "Indifference is worse than rejection."

Advice for Friends and Family

1. Touch them.
2. Make a loving gesture.
3. Quit asking.
4. Remember, it is not about you.
5. Read the newspaper.
6. Think before you speak.

Adapted from 15

A particular type of job stress becoming more prominent is related to mothers moving in and out of the workplace. Currently, according to The Bureau of Labor and Statistics, both parents now work in the majority, 63.2% of homes, compared to 29.5% where the father alone works.[16] Some lessons learned from mothers that have been there include; first, focus on your kids. Work for the family. Enjoy your life. Second, expect a "gender flip." In the roles between mom and dad, be versatile. Third, rebalance your life and then do it again. It may take awhile to strike the proper balance. Fourth, patience pays. Don't make sudden decisions on moving, house sale, and the like.

Mom in the Workplace

1. Focus on kids.
2. Expect "gender flip."
3. Rebalance your life.
4. Patience pays.

Adapted from 16

Some employee stressors can be related to normal growth and development such as pregnancy, illness or aging. Particular skill may be required for a successful job search while pregnant. Most experts suggest honesty during the interview process.

Tips for pregnant job seekers are offered by Dr. Linda Klau of New York; Marion Franklin, Tarrytown, New York; and Debra Brown, Long Beach, New York.[17] They suggest that first, project your life forward one year and design your work environment around it. Second, know definitively how much time you plan to take off. Third, do not present pregnancy as a problem. It is a non-issue. Fourth, bring pregnancy up once to your hiring contact, but not to each person in the interview process. Fifth, discuss your plan for maternity leave during the interview. Sixth, most importantly, dealing with the projected workload, in fact providing your employer with coverage solutions, may prove invaluable during your absence.

Baby on Board

1. Design your work environment around life one year from now.
2. Know how much time you plan to take off.
3. Pregnancy is not a problem. It is a non-issue.
4. Discuss the pregnancy once but not with each person.
5. Discuss maternity leave plans in the interview.

6. Provide your employer workload solutions while you are away.

Source: Dr. Linda Klau, Marion Franklin, and Debra Brown
Adapted from 17

Pride in your work may be over billed. A recent survey performed by Katsenburg Partners shows that approximately one half, or 47%, of younger (25-34 year old) workers agreed with the assessment that "feeling proud of your work is more important than getting a raise."[18] Interestingly, however, this phenomenon does not extend to older, more experienced workers. Here only one quarter, 25%, of middle-aged workers aged 45-54 and 20% of older workers, over 55, put pride above compensation.

In summary, these attributes can be focused into an adaptive strategy by incorporating these techniques. First, knowing when to draw the line can preserve your sanity. Second, try not to take things too personally. Third, attempt to broaden your life roles, incorporating family recreational issues, as well as increasing your level of volunteerism. Fourth, cultivate positive and productive mental habits using exercises and recreation, not smoking or dietary excess. Fifth, you will encounter dilemmas so develop positive coping strategies. Sixth, try not to get diffuse—focus on the problem at hand. Lastly, keep your workload in check to optimize both your time at work and your time at home.

Adaptive Strategy

1. Know when to draw the line.
2. Try not to take things too personally.
3. Attempt to broaden your life role.
4. Cultivate positive and productive mental habits.
5. You will encounter dilemmas—develop positive coping strategies.
6. Try not to get diffuse—stay in focus.
7. Keep your workload in check.

References

1. "Did You Know . . ." *Physician's Money Digest*. 30 September 2001.
2. "Weekly Wages." *Parade Magazine*. 25 February 2001, page 6.
3. Bureau of Labor Statistics, 2000.
4. Krantz, Les. *Jobs Related Almanac*. Barricade Books, 2002.
5. Drake, Beam and Morin, Outplacement Survey. 5 March 2002.
6. "Pink Slip for the Boss." *Business Week*. 1 April 2002, page 12.
7. Lublin, Joann S. "Mergers Often Trigger Anxiety, Lower Morale." *Wall Street Journal*. 16 January 2001. B1, 4.
8. Costello, Daniel. "Incidents of 'Desk Rage' Disrupt America's Offices." *Wall Street Journal*. 16 January 2001. B1, 4.
9. Shellenbarger, Sue. "Work and Family, Why You Can Hit the Gym-But Not Get a Manicure on Company Time." *Wall Street Journal*. 18 April 2002. B1.
10. Dobbin, Muriel. *McClatchy Newspapers*. Monica L Haynes. *Pittsburgh Post-Gazette*. "Everybody is Angry about Rude Behavior." 3 April 2002. A1, 9.
11. Hymowitz, Carol. "Impossible Expectations and Unfulfilling Work, Stress Managers II." *Wall Street Journal*. 16 January 2001.
12. Hymowitz, Carol and Rachel Silverman. "Can Workplace Stress Get Any Worse?" *Wall Street Journal*. 16 January 2001. B1-4.
13. Bureau of Labor Statistics, 2001.
14. Shellenbarger, Sue. "Work and Family, Call One Learning How to Work With the Good Stress, Live without the Bad." *Wall Street Journal*. 25 July 2001. B1.
15. Zaslo, Jeffrey. "Second Act Readers Share Job Loss Experience." *The Wall Street Journal*. 9 May 2002. D2.
16. Shellenbarger, Sue. "Work and Family; Please Send Chocolate. Moms Now Face Stress Moving In and Out of the Workforce." *Wall Street Journal*. 9 May 2002.
17. Dunham, Kemba J. "The Jungle; Focus on Recruitment, Pay and Getting Ahead." *Wall Street Journal*. 3 July 2002.
18. Katzenbach. "Take This Pride and Shove It." *Parker's Fortune Magazine*. 27 May 2002, page 188.

Chapter 13

Employee Development

In today's business world, the extensive variety of workplace endeavors finds a wide range of consumer likes and dislikes based on the occupational title alone. Historically, job titles such as physician ranked in the top three professions felt to be honorable.

However, the 2001 Gallup Poll was performed surveying 1,005 respondents after September 11th and, for the first time, includes security and public service professions.[1] In this summary; the most respected profession was firefighter, garnering 90% of the votes; followed by nursing with 84%. Interestingly, physicians and clergy dropped to 6th and 7th place respectively, in light of recent controversies for the latter.

Professions that were found least likely to be honest and ethical included insurance sales people, with a 13% rating; advertising executives, 11% and the car sales profession least likely (3%) to be respected.

The Most Honest and Ethical Professions

Top 7		Bottom 7	
Profession	Ranking (percentage)	Profession	Ranking (percentage)
Firefighter	90	Auto Mechanic	22
Nurse	84	Stock Broker	19
U. S. Military	81	Lawyer	18
Police Officer	68	Labor Union Leader	17
Pharmacist	68	Insurance Sales People	13
Doctor	66	Advertising Executive	11
Clergy	64	Car Sales People	3

Adapted from 1

Assuming things, as they are, some positions will inherently be better tolerated by some individuals than others we will then have to address focusing on job issues that can be targeted for improvement resulting in increased employee satisfaction.

In addition, it is understood that today's business needs are more than just an altruistic motive to improve the worker's lot. It should be obvious that flowing directly from happier, more content workers is the likelihood of delivery of a better, more efficient day's work, resulting directly in improved customer satisfaction.

On the other hand, there are both direct and indirect costs of unhappy employees. The most important direct cost is that associated with the prospects of employee turnover, which is often not considered, especially in large organizations.

Consultants, including Sibson & Company of Lexington and Nextera Enterprises, have studied employee turnover extensively and concluded that employers spend $75 million annually to replace more than 6.5 million employees who leave the 100 million person workforce each year.[2] The annual turnover rate in entry level jobs ranges from 31% in call centers to as many as 123% in the fast food industry. In the later sample, it is obvious that they must train 1.2 employees to stay for one year in that industry. Certainly, they would be considered short-term.

This data compares to the accepted human resources benchmark of 15-20% average annual turnover, with a floor turnover of 10% considered inevitable. However, there may, in fact, be a paradoxical effect where too low an employee turnover, i.e. 10% of less, may not be a desirable effect. If no one leaves the job, it may be too cushy in terms of job conditions, salary, benefits or work required.

Likewise, there is a wide range of financial implications associated with job turnover. The costs of retraining vary from a low of $1,520 annually for a fast food worker, to $10,445 for mid-point specialty retail staff, to a high of $34,100 for an information systems technology company employee.

Turnover: The Likelihood and Costs

	Turnover (%)	Costs ($)
Programmer or systems analyst		$34,100
Sales clerk		$10,445
Call center	31	$6,926
Fast food	123	$1,520

Adapted from 2

Therefore, it is incumbent upon every employer to continually analyze work conditions and compensation to ensure a climate of healthy turnover. Ideally, this rate should be between 10 and 15%, allowing the appropriate influx of new ideas, while avoiding the complacency and the stagnation of not being able to terminate a sub-optimal employee or having to tolerate poor work production.

Trust in the workplace has eroded since the early 1980's due to the "Wall Street type" buyouts, takeovers and acquisitions as well as the blistering rate of change independent of this fact.

There was a study of 1,800 workers, which was released by Aon's Loyalty Institute from Ann Arbor, Michigan that suggested that 1 in every 8 employees, or 13% overall, distrust their employers on a basic level and these workers are subject to fear, intimidation or harassment in the workplace.[3] They went as far as to suggest that trust is so basic a cornerstone to employee satisfaction that without it, no other benefits are sufficient to overwhelm this deficit.

Similarly, a study by Watson Wyatt Worldwide of Bethesda, Maryland, who studied over 7,500 employees concluded that only one half had trust in their senior management. They found a more basic pecuniary linkage between trust and profit. Specifically, shareholder returns were 42% in companies, where trust between labor and management was found.

The non-starter approach would be to ensure that it is impossible to cultivate an environment of trust in the setting of constant change, reorganization or upheaval. According to David Stum of the Loyalty Institute,[3] it is possible to establish and maintain an environment of trust as workers realize change is inevitable, but it is how you adapt and handle the change that matters. He suggests, first, that it is possible to cultivate trust in times of change as the employees believe in the basic principles involved. Second, it is certainly the small personal gestures that matter—a kind word or a note of appreciation, congratulations or condolences. Third, there can be no trust without the truth. It is the basis for all subsequent encounters.

Cultivate Trust in Times of Change

1. Believe in the idea.
2. Small gestures matter.
3. "Tell the truth" maxim.
4. What you would "teach your kids" philosophy.

Adapted from 3

A cogent summary of this concept is offered in *Trust and Betrayal in the Workplace*, a 1999 publication by Dennis and Michelle Reina.[4] They suggested the optimal workplace model to include, first, respecting others is the key to a functional workplace and the basis of trust. Second, the process of sharing information helps to progress towards to maximal efficiency, diminishing multiple redundant discussions in context. Third, mistakes do happen. You will make them and admitting responsibility is a huge positive public relations maneuver—as taking responsibility is the honorable thing to do and improves your position as viewed by workers and superiors alike.

Fourth, the use of constructive feedback is the basis for your continuous quality improvement process. Fifth, the premise of keeping secrets related to workplace activity is one of the most divisive maneuvers encountered. Eliminating "need to know information" categories will go a long way to improving employee buy-in and teamwork. Sixth, along these lines, workers avoiding personal gossip and backbiting in the work environment avoids their detrimental effect on employee morale.

Seventh, the process of consistency with objective goals and reinforcers improves efficiency in that employees are no longer afraid to make decisions, avoiding the variability of each individual supervisor. Lastly, no intervention promotes teamwork more effectively than to involve others in operational decision-making.

Trust and Betrayal in the Workplace

1. Respect others.
2. Share information.
3. Admit mistakes.

4. Constructive feedback.
5. Don't keep secrets.
6. Avoid gossip and backbiting.
7. Be consistent.
8. Involve others in decision-making.

Adapted from 3

Likewise, the surest way to make employees untrustworthy is "distrust them," which is attributed to Henry Stimpson, who served as Franklin Delano Roosevelt's Secretary of War.[4] The act of betrayal most certainly has a powerful adverse emotional effect on work performance, as well as secondary effects on the family and home life. This "distrust model" was illustrated by Bart Rhoten who described his experience in the credit card unit of a banking concern, employing such adversarial techniques as not authorizing overtime unless a supervisor was present, terminating those who returned late from lunch and promoting only from outside the company under the auspices of lack of respect for internal promotions by former coworkers, as the rationale. The result of this badly demoralized operation was a 400% turnover in a 300-person employee pool. A twenty-fold increase over the national average.[3]

The "Distrust Model"

1. Employees are not empowered to make the simplest decisions.
2. Do not allow them to make any financial decisions.
3. Threaten job security for minor infractions.
4. Promote only from outside the company.

The "Trust Model" was offered by Reinas Consultants of Stowe, Vermont, relating the story of a manufacturing plant in a small New England town where about one-quarter of the employees, 100 of 420 workers, were subject to a layoff.

Their strategy to deal with this problem included holding a meeting and sharing information face-to-face. The information was presented to all shifts and employees anytime of the day or night, answering all questions honestly and listening to their concerns. Lastly, they took an active interest in down-staffed employees, creating an outplacement center and an active marketing plan to broker other employees' interests in those whom were laid off.

The "Trust Model"
1. Meet to share information.
2. Present information to all employees.
3. Answer questions.
4. Listen to concerns.
5. Broker outside interest in your employees.

There has recently been a change in the employee-customer relationship in some industries where employees are becoming harder to find. Formerly, in the 1980's "the customer was king"—emphasizing such approaches as "the customer is key, the customer drives quality, the customer is the final judge, and the infamous "the customer is always right."

The new approach is to suggest that the relationship is not worth keeping if it drives the employees nuts. You should always love your client but you should love your coworkers and family more, according to Jack Valancy, a Medical Practice Management consultant. How do you decide who the bad clients are and which are the ones your company should bid farewell?

Employee-Client Relations

1980's	New
Customer:	Relationship not worth keeping:
1. is king.	1. Love your clients.
2. drives quality.	2. Love your coworkers more.
3. is the final judge.	3. Love your family most.
4. is always right.	

Several professional service consultants and firms, including R. Randall Brandt, senior V.P. from Burke Incorporated, a Cincinnati based consulting firm; Plante & Moran, a Southfield, Michigan accounting firm; and John Garrigan of Barton Protective Services all offered these suggestions on which clients to fire.[5]

They suggest that you should terminate clients who are inherently detrimental to the operation including, first, those with an arrogant "all about me" attitude. Second, those who adversely impact an employee's quality of life issues at work or home; third, those who are particularly burdensome or detrimental to staff morale, and lastly, those who damage worker productivity. You might ask, how would business goals be advanced by eliminating clients, your revenue lifeblood? The answer is that maintaining troublesome and less loyal customers in the system is clearly less profitable, ultimately increasing system costs, not increasing revenue overall.

What Clients to Lose

1. Arrogant "all about me" attitude."
2. Affect quality of life issues.
3. Damage worker productivity.
4. Detrimental to morale.
5. Troublesome customers are less profitable and less loyal.

This information culminates in an action plan to aid your career development[6,7] offered by Ellig & Morin in their book, *What Every Successful Woman Knows, 12 Breakthrough Strategies to Get Power and Ignite Your Career*, related by Toddi Gunter. First, take stock of where you are currently and help to set future goals. Second, try to fit in and adapt before you initiate change so staff will be more likely buy in. Third, ensure the importance of your job and that your responsibility, including a profit and loss relationship for the business concern.

Fourth, try to develop mutually useful and helpful relationships with your bosses to eliminate unnecessary friction in your job performance. Fifth, create your own power base both inside and outside the corporation to improve your bargaining position. Sixth, speak your mind but be relevant—offer timely, helpful suggestions. Seventh, build your own brand name and promote yourself by tooting your own horn a lot.

Eighth, devote your time to significant projects. Try not to waste time on irrelevant issues. Ninth, devote the majority (80%) of your time performing your job responsibilities and the minority (20%) to career management. The sure way to not advance your career is to worry more about your promotion than about doing your actual job, according to Alisa Zimmel of Takeda Pharmaceuticals Company.[8] Tenth, the clear way to career advancement is to maximize your technical, business, and people skills. Eleventh, be wise and careful to avoid office romance. If you do become involved, be especially cognizant and establish sexual harassment procedures and customary social protocols. Lastly, act with authority—establish a plan to communicate your vision, take risks and make things happen.

Action Plan for Your Career

1. Take stock of where you are and set future goals.
2. Fit in and adapt before you initiate change.
3. Ensure that your job has "profit and loss" responsibility.
4. Develop mutually useful relationships with your supervisors.
5. Create your own power base both inside and outside the corporation.
6. Speak your mind but be relevant.
7. Build your brand name recognition and toot your own horn.
8. Spend time on significant projects.
9. Devote 80% of your time performing your job and 20% attending to career management.
10. Maximize your technical, business and people skills.
11. Be wise about office romance issues. Follow established sexual harassment procedures.
12. Act with authority.
    a. Communicate division.
    b. Take risks.
    c. Make things happen.

Adapted from 6

Ideally, the best employees can be interpreted to be *"energy suppliers"* who don't have all the answers but have solutions—"leave it me, I'll find out why." Ultimately, face your mistakes if they occur. Fix it and move on.[9] You certainly don't want to be classified as an energy drainer, a worrier, more shadow than substance or feel drained by the end of the conversation.

The Balance of Energy Suppliers	**Drainer**
Not all the answers, but seeks a solution	Worrier
Leave it to me	More shadow than substance
Fix problems and move on	Feel drained by the end of the conversation

Adapted from 9

The last issue raised is assuming you believe you have done excellent work, so how do you get a raise? Suzanne Koudsi compiled this list of consultants who offer this advice, when you desire a raise during lean economic times.[10] These recommendations include a plan to first design your own incentives, according to Fred Crandall from The Center for Workplace Effectiveness. If your company needs to cut costs, design the plan and benefit from the augmented revenues. Second, look beyond your checking account, according to Paula Todd of Towers Perrin. Be amenable to non-cash awards, flex time or extra vacation time.

Thirdly, don't ignore your career development as promotional opportunities may be priceless, even without increased compensation. The likelihood of a delayed pay-off is increased in your subsequent job market looking for employment as a V.P. rather than a lesser manager. Fourth, think before you speak. There may be a reason that your raise was not forthcoming. Be introspective, your performance may not have warranted advancement, according to Frank Belmonte of Hewitt Associates. Likewise, go in with objective data. Determine what goals are required to advance, achieve those goals and present your performance objectives convincingly, says Steven Gross of Mercer Human Resource Consulting.

Fifth, always stay focused on the future, according to Dan Moynihan of Compensation Resources. You should consider delayed gratification alternatives, such as asking for a financial commitment at some defined future date. Position yourself at the top of the heap so that if any funds become available they will go to you or substitute a bonus for a raise as the long-term financial commitment is less for the company.

Sixth, open your mind to alternative offers or perks, according to Paula Todd. Ask what the company could offer to improve your piece of mind without costing more money—a better office, a parking space or a title change. Remember, the later can always be brokered for more compensation on the back-end of a job change scenario.

Seventh, be flexible and look for ways to shift or reallocate work or expenses. There may be a need for fewer personnel, out-sourcing or a more efficient operational mode that could ultimately save money for the corporation.

Lastly, don't be a hot head. Thoughts and ideas that benefit the company first, and you second are more likely to be successful than a "what's in it for me" strategy.[11]

Getting the Raise

1. Design your own incentives.
2. Look beyond your checking account.
3. Don't ignore career development.
4. Think before you speak.
5. Focus on the future.
6. Open your mind.
7. Be flexible.
8. Don't get hot headed.

Adapted from 11

The business market had a flat year for raises and incentive pay. Following a December, 2001 study of 143 large businesses, Towers Perrin, a New York based salary consulting firm suggested that 59% of the businesses reduce their 2002 merit increase budgets to increases of 3.5% or less, compared to that same proportion of 4% or higher in 2001.[12]

Suggestions that were offered to help negotiate a pay raise include, first, look for objective signs that your company is in a recovery mode.[12] Second, speak with others outside your company who have successfully obtained a raise in their industry for helpful tips. Third, monitor the Internet web sites that are specific to your industry and region to allow an accurate prediction of your earning potential. Fourth, always approach your manager in-person when discussing a potential pay raise. Fifth, make a productive counteroffer by seeking an alternative job position.

Tips for Negotiating a Pay Raise

1. Assess whether your employer is in a recovery mode.
2. Talk to others outside the company to elicit successful strategies.
3. Monitor Internet sites with industry- and region-specific salaries.
4. Discuss raise issues in-person with your manager.
5. Seriously seek another job and counteroffer to your current employer.
6. Focus on team, not individual performance that benefits the company.

Adapted from 11

"We are using an industrial age model emphasizing equipment in a knowledge age world, which should emphasize people," according to Stephen Covey.[12] Workers are less productive than they could be due to antiquated management style de-emphasizing initiative and creativity, focusing on fine-tuning efforts rather than innovative models. The key to significant development is to affect not just behavior and attitude focused on minor change, but to affect a paradigm shift by changing the employee role.

Attempt to minimize the amount of counterproductive activity. Franklin Covey Research suggests that 75% of workers spend one quarter of their time on CYA communication conflicts dealing with hidden agendas, while 25% rate this activity as much as half of the workplace endeavors. Rather than using the dictatorial approach of managing employees, let them manage themselves by helping to develop policy.

Knowledge Age Management—People Not Equipment

1. Emphasize people, not equipment.
2. Paradigm shift, not fine-tuning or micromanagement.
3. Minimize counterproductive activity.
4. Let employees manage themselves.

Adapted from 12

Perhaps, most importantly, your worth to the company as a team player, improving their overall performance, is more significant than your individual attributes, and that makes you indispensable to the company.

References

1. "Honest and Ethical Profession." Gallup Organization. November 2001. *Physician's Money Digest*. 31 January 2002, page 30.
2. "Turnover Costs." Sibson and Company. Nextera Enterprises. *Wall Street Journal*. 2001.
3. Shellenbarger, Sue. "Work and Family, Workplace Upheavals Seem to be Eroding Employees Trust." *Wall Street Journal*. 2000. B1
4. Reina, Dennis S. and Michelle L. Reina. *Trust and Betrayal in the Workplace*. Berret-Koehler Publishers, First Edition, 1999.

5. Shellenbarger, Sue. "Work and Family, More Firms Siding With Employees, Bid Bad Clients Farewell." *Wall Street Journal.* 2000. B1
6. Gutner, Toddi. "A Twelve Step Program to Gaining Power." *Business Week.* 21 December 2001, page 88.
7. Ellig, Janice and William J. Morin. *What Every Successful Woman Knows, 12 Breakthrough Strategies to Get the Power to Ignite Your Career.* McGraw Hill, New York, 2001.
8. Zimmel, Alisa. Takeda Pharmaceuticals Co. Personal Communication. 2002.
9. Shallenbarger, Sue. "Working Family." *Wall Street Journal.* 25 July 2001.
10. Koudsi, Susan. "You Want More." *Fortune Magazine.* 29 April 2002, pages 177-178.
11. Dunham, Kemba J. "The Jungle-Focus on Recruitment, Pay and Getting Ahead." *Wall Street Journal.* 23 April 2002. B8.
12. Murphy, Dave. "When Happy Workers? Change the Rules." *San Francisco Chronicle* reprinted in the *Pittsburgh Post Gazette.* 6 June 2002.

Chapter 14

Best "Business Practice" Companies

There appears to be some positive trends offered in both good and bad times. There are other factors often more important than salary, benefits or vacation.

Perhaps, the most critical consideration of the company best practice is the importance of "open communication," according to Judy Olian, Dean of Penn State's Smeal College of Business, who specializes in human resources management.[1] The best companies offer their employees the chance to participate in decision-making, whether good or bad. The company usually benefits when employees are given the ability to create policy, explore new markets and provide efficiency strategies. Employees are especially motivated to trade cost-cutting for jobs and participate when given a forum in a retreat or given an "open door" policy to company executives.

Second, employee perceptions are significantly influenced by the values and ideals of leadership. The company is viewed more favorably if they are actively participating in charitable and community concerns. The benefit profile can be quite helpful in profiling a favorable company. These added benefits could take the form of free products, child care, fitness facilities, vacation or educational benefits. Be cautious, however, that these are truly added value benefits and they do not impact negatively on financial remuneration. Fourth, these programs tend to be unsuccessful if viewed as short-term or gimmicky, and are more likely to be embraced if they are a direct extension of company ideals. The success of a program, such as this suggests that investing in your most precious asset, your employees, gives the best long-term return on investment.

Good Company Practice

1. Open communication.
2. Leadership values.
3. Benefit profile.
4. Extension of principles.
5. Invest in your most precious asset, people.

Adapted from 1

The advent of change is often disheartening and demoralizing for employees in the trenches and no matter how ingenious a plan, a new strategy will fail without support of the rank and file. Derived from these two observations is the fact that the time spent on creating the support base is more crucial than the actual operations phase in better companies.

Carol Hymowitz relates the experience of W. James McNerney, CO of 3M Company, who assumed the helm of this diverse manufacturing company, implementing difficult programs such as a 10% job cut and the infamous six sigma process management system that isolates tasks to small increments measured against the perfect model achieving 99.9999% reliability.[2] Initially, this black and white data-driven strategy went over like a lead balloon in this small town, collegially-administered company. The new cooperative approach began with a casual retreat to first reformulate core values by charting the course, energizing and inspiring others and delivering results. Second, ask for employee help with a problem. Don't dictate. Third, modify aggressive employee policies like objective rating scales to translate perks for better-than-average employees. Fourth, value leadership as much as you do experience, allowing employees to perform out of their narrow areas.

Implementing Change

1. Open forum.
2. Reformulate core values.
   a. Chart the course.
   b. Energize and inspire others.
   c. Deliver results.
3. Ask for help with a problem, don't dictate.
4. Modify an incentives rating policy.
5. Value leadership as well as experience.

Adapted from 2

The best companies concentrate on ensuring all aspects of their employees' work and home life balance. A particularly emotive area is the relationship between an employee's spouse and their boss. In contrast to days gone by, the spousal entertaining function of co-mingling has been replaced with brief, cold, formal encounters masking household tensions and hidden agendas, according to Sue Shellenbarger, who offers these tips.[3]

First, establish solid home/work boundaries to keep tensions and undercurrents from spilling over to the family situation. Second, agree upon pre-established conversational ground rules before your spouse and boss meet. Third, if there is prior tension, avoid face-to-face meetings to avoid a confrontation unless absolutely necessary. Fourth, be introspective and ask yourself, "is the tension related to deeper problems in your marriage and not work related?" Fifth, agree on a time limit to propose and implement solutions for resolving the conflict.

Preventing Spousal and Boss Conflict

1. Set good home/work boundaries.
2. Agree on conversational ground rules.
3. Avoid face-to-face confrontational meetings.
4. Be introspective-is the tension on your end?
5. Set a time limit for conflict resolution.

Adapted from 3

Forward thinking businesses realize the crucially important spousal interface and can determine if the proper employee will take the job, how long they will stay, and their satisfaction level.

Employer concern transcends the person and applies to the physical work environment, as well. Jay Grand, a cognitive psychologist employed by Hayworth Incorporated, a Michigan based furniture manufacturer, spends his day trying to avoid the Dilbert "rat in a cage" design so commonplace in today's office environment.[3]

Historically, problems with the design began with the railroad industry in the 1800's where 100s of clerks may have be housed in an open bullpen environment surrounded by the din of adding machines and typewriters with an isolated boss' office at the head. A breath of fresh air arrived in the 1950's when the "Burolandschaft" or German office landscape movement took hold; emphasizing an open, organic design with free flow between management and worker. However, almost immediately this plan was forced into a territorial environment by developers and managers to conserve space—the "cubicle" movement, as it persists to this day.

Cataloging the most popular choices amongst employees includes, first, a window view as most people do not like to stare at a "blank wall." Second, they like a "symmetrically lit" office with a floor covered with variable lighting levels. Third, they do not like loud noise or distractions but similarly do not like total silence as well. Lastly, the "closed" environment is felt to be less stressful than the "open" environment.

Success is measured by the productivity and impact on the occupants of the office "landscape." The typical noise level is indeed higher in "open" office settings manifesting in adverse impact by increasing stress and decreasing motivational levels.

Brand cites a crucial point in that 82% of a company's costs over a 10-year period are employee based, while only 5% are related to the real estate. Therefore, relatively small financial expenditures in design and structure can have long lasting employee benefits in both productivity and longevity.

Optimum Office Design

1. Exterior light windows.
2. Symmetrically lit space.
3. Decrease noise and distraction.
4. Avoid total silence.
5. "Closed" over "open" environment.
6. Success measured as occupant impact.

Adapted from 4

Designing employee-friendly environments extends to aesthetic appeal items; such as color scheme, where references can be extrapolated from the web design plan of Thomas Muller, VP for experience design, at New York-based Razorfish.[4]

Their color scheme incorporates "blue" found in older, tradition laden companies stressing stability as the safest and most understood color design favoring financial service sites such as American Express, Ford, and IBM. Green, especially in softened shades can have a calming effect on the individual. It has been felt to project youthfulness and the prospect of growth. Red is an attention getting color, signifying passion, celebrations of love, and attracting attention. White is associated with purity and innocence creating a "sense of pristineness" for an affluent audience. Black may convey dark and negative qualities. However, on the positive side it can symbolize strength and reliability by speaking with "authority and power." On the cultural side, it is associated with formality and sophistication associated with high fashion. Although these color references relate to the electronic media environment, the proper or innovative use of color can help the environment, as well.

Color Design

Color		Firms
1. Blue	"Safest and most well understood"	IBM
	"all about stability"	Ford
	"traditional and older"	American Express
2. Green	"calming effect"	First Union
	"youthfulness and growth"	Origins
3. Red	"creates attention"	Cadence & Wesleyan
	"passion, celebration and love"	
	"attention, call to action"	
4. White	"purity and innocence"	Yahoo!
	"cool and refreshing"	Clinique
	"sense of pristineness"	
	"affluence"	
5. Black	"dark and negative"	Barney &
	"strength and reliability"	Maccomestics
	"authority and power"	
	"formality and sophistication"	

Adapted from 5

Perhaps the most important area for employers to exhibit concern for their workers is in the area of state of health. The National Center of Health Statistics suggested that 70% of adults didn't exercise regularly and 40% had no physical activity whatsoever.[6] Likewise, a federal government survey performed in 2000 suggested that over half the population (56.4%) were overweight with this figure most recently revised up to 61%, replacing tobacco as the number one health care problem resulting in greater health claims and absenteeism.

Progressive companies have realized the benefits of proactive health plans including diet and exercise, which have been realized in decreased absenteeism and healthcare costs.

Alexander R. Moses found a wide range of programs offered in today's corporate environment. General Motors offers yoga, tae chi classes above the assembly line in Flint, Michigan. Union Pacific Railroad offers a rolling fitness center. Chrysler offers free incentive bonuses for leisure or health-related activities. Cigna offers a weight management program to 1,000 people who lost an average of 10 to 15 lbs. last year.

They suggest that roughly half of the companies with 750 employees or greater offer a comprehensive employee health promotion program. These programs are felt to be strong recruiting tools for your personnel who tend to have healthier life habits than their predecessors.

Today, as individuals claim more responsibility for their own health—issues such as prevention and workplace wellness become more prominent. Joe S. Meredith, president of West Virginia Wellness Network, offered these suggestions on a corporate wellness program that provides these benefits; including, first, approved health status.[7] Second, health care cost containment. Third, improved morale. Fourth, reduced turnover and absenteeism.

Corporate Wellness Benefits

1. Improved health status.
2. Health care cost containment.
3. Improved morale.
4. Reduced turnover.
5. Reduced absenteeism.

Adapted from 7

The suggestions to start an effective employee wellness program include a plan to first obtain the support of senior management. Second, establish health as a priority. Third, develop a "work point of wellness" committee. Fourth, assess organizational and employee needs. Fifth, construct an operating plan.[7]

Employee Wellness Plan
1. Senior management support.
2. Health is a priority.
3. Appoint wellness committee.
4. Assess organizational employee needs.
5. Operating plan.

Adapted from 7

Hopefully, the benefits extend from the employee to the business owner, as well due to better health and productivity.

References

1. Olian, Judy. "On the Job, Good Companies Have One Thing in Common, An Ear for Their Employees." *Pittsburgh Post-Gazette*. 9 April 2002. D7.
2. Hymowitz, Carol. "In the Lead, How a Leader at 3M Got His Employees to Back Big Changes." *Wall Street Journal*. 23 April 2002. B1.
3. Shellenbarger, Sue. "Work and Family 'Help! My Spouse Hates My Boss: A Whole New Kind of Love Triangle." *Wall Street Journal*. 11 April 2002. D1.
4. Fitzpatrick, Dan. "Building Happiness. Psychologist Helps Design Offices Where Employees Want to Work." *Pittsburgh Post-Gazette*. 23 April 2002. E1 and E2.
5. Muller, Thomas. "Shades of Meaning." *Wall Street Journal*. 15 April 2002. D1 and 6.
6. Moses, Alexandra R. "Employers Find Ways to Encourage Good Health." *Pittsburgh Post-Gazette*. 23 April 2002. E2
7. Meredith, Joe S. and Patricia Lake. "Why West Virginia Needs Work Site Wellness." *WV Executive*. Spring 2002, pages 17-21.

Chapter 15

Prologue

Although today's work is not analogous to that of the textile mills, mines and factories of years gone by, it is associated with it's own unique type of dysfunctional stress. Frank Lehner offers an analysis of Jill Andresky-Fraser's work, "The White Collar Sweat Shop and Deterioration of Work and its Rewards in Corporate America."[1] She describes the state of affairs where workers are disenfranchised and subjected to long work weeks, survive on diminished salaries and worsened benefits, work under increasing stress levels and ultimately sacrifice their home and financial lives for the workplace endeavor.[2] No, this isn't an industrial tale of the immigrant steelworkers laboring in *The Mill,* a tale told by Rade B. Vukmir a generation ago—this is 2003.[3]

The Disenchanted Worker

1. Disenfranchised.
2. Long workweek.
3. Diminished salary.
4. Worsened benefits.
5. Increasing stress.
6. Adverse home effects.

Adapted from 2

This position, in which we find ourselves, is the product of a 20-year proliferation of "slash and burn" management—attempting to maximize shareholder value.[3] The pace of corporate mergers from 1980 to 1990 found that 65-75% of companies lost value overall to a total of $90 billion while $20-25 billion was paid to investment bankers.

This resulted in the disillusion of the American Dream with workers too preoccupied with civil and social contributions now lost, destroying both local neighborhoods and a general sense of community. In addition, new productivity-enhancing technology allows for an inescapable "365/24/7 workplace" due to electronic media. The workers can expect nothing more except from themselves. They are the last to cling to an outmoded work ethic purported to be left by management long ago. The corporate mentality finds that loyalty may just be an illusion with job security a cultural artifact.

Certainly, the actual situation may not be as dire as predicted. There are tremendous new opportunities for development and growth in the new economy—bringing traditional work ethics to new ideas. However, life is stressful. The former work ethic is gone and unprecedented rates of job disability and poor performance abound, as well as no corporate loyalty or obligation.

References

1. Lehner, Frank. "The Payoff for Hard Work Isn't What It Used to Be." *Pittsburgh Post-Gazette*. 11 March 2001.
2. Andresky-Fraser, Jill. *White Collar Sweat Shop—The Deterioration of Work and It's Rewards in Corporate America*. W. W. Norton and Company. First Edition, 2001.
3. Vukmir, Rade B. *The Mill*. University Press of America. Lanham, Maryland. First Edition, 1999.

Chapter 16

Conclusion

Even in the old version of the analogy where the customer is right 99% of the time, but is not right 1% of the time, does not allow chasing this 1% to be detrimental to the staff and operations in general. The management should establish realistic goals and objectives allowing the staff a reasonable chance of achieving them. According to Tom Zguris, MD, MBA, of Emergency Consultants, Inc., the best way to retain clients is to, as well, continually seek new ones due to ebb and flow in the business.[1] Protect your client base, but protect your staff, as well.

Remember, the 5 to 9 rule—5 people will relate a good encounter but 9 will relate a bad. Your message should be concise, compelling and most importantly the truth, according to Lindy Lazar Marketing, represented by Cathy Nelson and Karen Soderholm.[2]

The Message

1. Concise.
2. Compelling.
3. The truth.

Adapted from 2

It is critical to know the model in which you operate. The private sector is one in which the market drives a decrease in price and increase in service offered, while a governmental or monopoly market may operate with a fixed or increased price and service decrease as things gets tough.

Performance is equivalent to service divided by expectations ($P=S/E$). Therefore, increased performance can be achieved by offering increased service, as well as setting realistic expectations. The most effective approach is to, first, believe in something or someone bigger than yourself, according to Retired Lieutenant General Harold G. Moore. Second, selfless devotion to the principle will help you succeed. Third, there is nothing more integral than the work ethic. Fourth, elevate your coworkers to a position above your own.

Again, never stop until your objective is achieved. Strive to get what you want, take what you can get, and don't hold out for unrealistic expectations. You must control the game as much as possible to succeed.

The Keys to Success

1. Believe in something or someone greater than yourself.
2. Selfless devotion to a principle.
3. Work ethic above all else.
4. Put your coworkers above yourself.
5. Never stop until the objective is achieved.

Lastly, the most likely cause of discontent is the presence of unrecognized achievement—either not recognized at all or having credit for that activity taken by a superior. The best approach is to acknowledge contribution to achievement and reward solid effort with praise. Success is not always necessary but trying to the best of your potential is.

In this day of perception of CEO greed, corporate fraud and decreasing investor confidence, returning to our starting point will serve us well. The simple and honest work ethic of your parents, grandparents or great-grandparents should carry the day.

References

1. Zguris, Tom. "Personal Communication 2000."
2. Lindy Lazar Marketing, Cathy Nelson and Karen Soderholm. "Marketing Presentation." 27 April 2002.
3. Moore, Harold G. and Joseph J. Galloway. *We Were Soldiers Once . . . and Young: Ia Drang—The Battle That Changed the War in Vietnam.* Random House, First Edition, 1992. Mass Market Paperback, Reprint, 2000.

Index

3M Company, 98

Abercrombie and Fitch™, 67
absenteeism, 101–102
Acheson, Bill, 13
achievement leadership, 21, 22
acquisitions and mergers, 59; and effect on employees, 73
adverse experiences, 62–63
aggressiveness, 17
Altfest, Lewis J., PhD, 52–53
American Customer Satisfaction (ACSI) Index, 53–54
American Express, 100–101
American Son, the Story of John F. Kennedy, Jr., 34
Andresky-Fraser, Jill, 105
Anger Institute, 74
AOL-Time Warner, Inc., 53
Aon's Loyalty Institute, 87
Apollo, 38
Apollo 13, 38
Apollo I, 38
ArtKraft, 6
Atlas, Teddy, 44

Bain and Company, 55–56
Balmer, Steve, 66–67
Baranowski, Mitch, 62
Barton Protective Services, 90–91
Belmonte, Frank, 93

benefits, 23–24. *See also* compensation; incentives
Bertolli, North America, 19
best "business practice" companies, 97–103; and employee wellness benefits and plans, 102–103; and good company practices, 97–98; and implementation of change, 98; and prevention of spousal/boss conflict, 99; and work environments, 99–103
Blanson, David, 19–20
Blattner-Brunner, 45
Blechschmidt, Edward A., 29
Blewitt, Rich, 65
Blow, Richard, 34
body language, 13
Bonsignore, Michael, 30
boss/spouse conflict, 99
Boswell, Wendy, 79
Boudreau, John, 79
"boundless energy", 32
Bowen, Brayton R., 74
boxing model, 44
Brandt, R. Randall, 90–91
Bridger, Barbara, 11
British Rail system, 18
Brown, David R., 73
Brown, Debra, 81–82
Brown, Richard H., 27
Buckingham, Marcus, 25–26

Burke Incorporated, 90–91
"business is combat" model, 37–38
business models, 37–46. *See also specific model*; and boxing, 44; "captain of the ship" model, 45; Customer Relationship with Management model (CRM model)™, 41–42; and factory line approach, 46; and information technology, 41–42; medical model, 40–41; military model, 37–38; NASA model, 38; performance model, 42–44; sports model, 38–40; and thoroughbred horse racing, 45–46
business plan: development of, 10–11; model for, 9–10
business start-up, 9–11; errors in, 9–10
business success, 49–56. *See also* business models; Lewis J. Alfest's views on, 52–53; and American Customer Satisfaction (ACSI) Index, 53–54; Steve Case's views on, 53; and CEOs' succession, 54–56; John Chambers' views on, 50–51; and core business, 55–56; employees' contributions to, 23–24; Bill Gates' views on, 49; Stephen Hardis' views on, 49–50; keys to, 108; and leadership traits, 21, 54–55; in managerial progression, 29–30; Medical Group Management Association's views on, 51–52; mothers' influences on, 19–20; reasons for, 17
business turnaround, 69–70
Butler Manufacturing, 11

Campbell, Don, 42–44
"captain of the ship" model, 45
Card, Andrew, 24
career development, 23–24. *See also* employee development; managerial development
Carnegie Institute, 17
Case, Steve, 53
The Center for Workplace Effectiveness, 92–93
CEOs: qualities sought in, 19; succession of, 54–56; success of, 53–54
CFI Group, 53
Chambers, John, 50, 59
change: environment of, 59–60; implementation of, 98; of jobs (turnover), 33; leadership and, 21, 22, 59–60; and trust and betrayal in the workplace, 87–90
Chaplin, W. F., 14–15
Chicago Bulls, 39–40
Christian and Timbers, 19
Chrysler, 69, 102
Cigna, 102
Cisco Systems, 50, 59
clients, elimination of troublesome, 90–91
color scheme, of work environments, 100–101
communication: and corporate development, 30–31; open, 97; and trust, 59
companies. *See also specific company*; and best "business practices", 97–103
Compaq Company, 61
compensation, 23–24, 92–94; and customer satisfaction, 59; and employee stressors, 71–72
Compensation Resources, 93
competition, 59–63; and adverse experience, 62–63; and bad

public relations, 62; maintenance of, 60–61; and managing change, 59–60; and managing through distraction, 61–62; with own customers, 2–3; and slumping economies, 60
continuous quality improvement (CQI), 42; and constructive feedback, 88–89
core business, business success and, 55–56
Cornell Center for Advanced Human Resource Studies, 79
Corning, 6
corporate makeovers, 67–68
Costello, Daniel, 74
Covey, Stephen, 95
Crandall, Fred, 92–93
"credibility gap", 1–2
crisis intervention, 62; negative, 65–66; positive, 65
crisis leadership/management, 65–70; and business turnaround, 69–70; and companies under siege, 66–67; and corporate makeovers, 67–68; and leadership during troubled times, 21, 22, 68–69; and negative intervention, 65–66; and positive intervention, 65; and restoring public trust, 65–66
culture building leadership, 21, 22
customer/client interaction, 13
Customer Relationship with Management model (CRM model)™, 41–42
customer service, and medical model, 40–41
Cvetic, Jimmy, 13

D'Amato, Gus, 44
decision-making ability, 23–24, 97
demotion, 31–32

DiCamillo, Gary, 54
Distinction Communication, 43
"distrust model", 89–90
diversification, of product quality, 2–3
Domino's Pizza, 19–20
Donnely, Kathleen Dixon, 80
Drake, Beam & Morin, 72
Duckworth, T. D., v

Eaton Corporation, 49–50
Eckerd Company, 29
economy, changes in, 60
Einstein, Albert, and three rules of work, 1
Electronic Data Systems, 27
Ellig, Janice, 91–92
Emergency Consultants, Inc., 13, 107
employee-client relations, 90–91
employee contribution, to business success, 23–24
employee development, 85–95; action plan for, 91–92; and company's emphasis on people, 95; and compensation and incentives, 92–94; and employee-client relations, 90–91; and energy suppliers and drainers, 92–93; and trust and betrayal in the workplace, 87–90; and turnover rates and costs, 86–87; and views of professions, 85–86
employee empowerment, 59
employee evaluation, 28
employee frustration, 77–78
employee loyalty, 34, 87–90
employee motivation, 32, 39–40, 42
employees. *See also specific issue*; and corporate mission, 10; disenchanted, 105–106; importance of, 11; skills sought in,

17–18; and turnover rates and costs, 86–87
employee satisfaction: leadership and, 20–21; and trust and betrayal in the workplace, 87–90
employee stressors, 71–82; adaptive strategies for, 79–80, 82; adverse effects of, 74; and aging, 81–82; and compensation, 71–72; and effects of workplace stress, 77–79; and employee frustration, 77–78; and good stress, bad stress model, 79; and illness, 81–82; and mothers moving in and out of the workplace, 80–81; and normal growth and development, 81–82; and pregnancy, 81–82; and pride in work, 82; and stress avoidance behavior, 75–76; warning signs of, 74–75; and work environments, 72
employee wellness benefits and plans, 102–103
employment layoff possibility, 33–34
empowerment, of employees, 59
Endicott, Jim, 43
energy suppliers and drainers, 92–93
environments, work. *See* work environments
equipment, versus people, 95
espirit de corps, 17
ESPN II, 44
Exelon Chicago Utility, 29
expectations: management of, 3; and performance, 107–108

factory line approach, 46
family succession, in businesses, 5–6
Federal Aviation Administration, 18
Federal-Mogul Corporation, 69
feedback, constructive, 88–89
Ferdada, Antonio, 6

financial traits, of winning companies, 52–53
Fink, Stephen, 65–66
Finkle, Paul, 78
Fiorina, Carly, 61
Firestone Tire, 65
flattery, 15
Florida International University, 80
focus: for future, 53; maintaining, 50–51
Ford Motor Company, 39, 100–101
formal business interaction, 13–14
Fornell, Claes, 54
'four "P" principle', 9
Franklin, Marion, 81–82
Franklin Covey Research, 95
front line leadership, 17

Gage, Guy, 21
Gallup Organization, 25–26
Gallup Poll, 85
The Gap™, 67
Garrigan, John, 90–91
Gates, Bill, 49
GCI Group, 65
General Electric Company, 19
General Electric Industrial Systems, 32
General Motors, 102
Gensia Biotechnology Research Firm, 40–41
Gentiva Health Services, 29
Glass, David, 54–55
Glenn, John, 38
good stress, bad stress model, 79
Gougelman, Paul, 5
Gougelman, Peter, 5
Gougelman, Pierre, 5
GOV Works™, 33
Grand, Jay, 99
Gross, Daniel, 5
Gross, Steven, 93
group mentality, 39–40

Index

Gruber, Harry, Dr., 40–41
Gunter, Toddi, 91–92

handshake, 14
Hardis, Stephen, 49–50
Harvard Business School, 77–78
Hayworth Incorporated, 99
health concerns, 101–102
Heinz Company, 32
Henry W. T. Mali and Company, 5
Hewitt Associates, 93
Hewlett Packard Company, 61
hiring strategies, 27. *See also* personnel development
history, of modern businesses, 5–6
HNC Software, 30
Honeywell, 30
Hopkins, Jim, 9–10
horse racing, thoroughbred, 45–46
Howland Group, 74
HRPath.com, 78
HR Solutions, 23
human engineering, 17–18
Hupp, Dan, 45
Hymowitz, Carol, 98

I. Venture Lab, 9
IBM, 100–101
idea implementation, 41–42
improvement potential, 1–2
incentives, 92–94. *See also* benefits; compensation
income. *See also* compensation; incentives; median weekly, 71–72
industrial age model, 95
informal conversation, 30–31
information technology, 49–50
information technology model, 41–42
integration, vertical and horizontal, 2–3
intellectual property, 9

J. C. Penney Drug Store, 29
Jackson, Phil, 39–40
Jeeter, Derrick, 38–39
Jensen, Michael C., 1–2
Jiminiz, D'Angelo, 38–39
job attributes, desirable, 23–24
job control, 23–24
job desirability, 72
job loss, 79–80; potential for, 72–73
job promotion, 29
job satisfaction, 23–24
job security, 23–24, 106
job tenure, 72–73
job turnover/change, 33
Johnson, James M., MD, PhD, 13, 45
Johnson, William, 32
Jones & Laughlin Steel Company, v
Journal of Personal and Social Psychology, 14–15

Kamber, Victor, 65–66
Kamber Group, 65–66
Katsenburg Partners, 82
Keiya Mizuno, 15
Kelley, Edward J., III, 30
Kentucky Derby, 45–46
Kessler, Andy, 2–3
Klau, Linda, Dr., 81–82
K-Mart, 54
Koehn, Nancy, 77–78
komegoroshi, 15
Koudsi, Suzanne, 92–93
Kozlowski, L. Dennis, 54
Kraines, Gerald, 77
Kramer, Larry, 65
Kranz, Gene, 38

layoff possibility, 33–34
leadership, 17–22; and achievement, 21, 22; and aggressiveness, 17; change and, 21, 22, 59–60; culture building, 21, 22; and

employee satisfaction, 20-21; and employee skills sought, 17-18; front line, 17; and human engineering, 17-18; and management styles, 20-21; millennial, 21, 22; and mothers' influences on success, 19-20; and positive supervisory attributes, 20-21; and qualities sought in CEOs, 19; succession, 21, 22; traits of successful, 21, 54-55; during troubled times, 21, 22, 68-69; types of, 21-22; values and ideals of, 97; visionary, 21, 22
Lehner, Frank, 105
leverage, of brand, 2-3
Levin, Jerry, 54
Levinson Institute, 77
Lexicon Communications Group, 65-66
The Limited™, 67
Lindy Lazar Marketing, 107
Lublin, Joann S., 33, 73
lying, reasons for, 1-2

Mali, Frederick, 5
Mali, Henry, 5
management. *See also* leadership; of change, 59-60; of a company under siege, 66-67; and concern for employees, 23-24; of realistic expectations, 3; through distraction, 61-62
management styles. *See also* leadership; affect of employee satisfaction on, 20-21
managerial development, 27-34; and "boundless energy", 32; and communication, 30-31; and employee loyalty, 34; and employee motivation, 32; and evaluation of employees, 28; and hiring strategies, 27; and job promotion, 29; and job turnover/change, 33; and layoff possibility, 33-34; and "managing up", 28-29; and planning for negative outcomes, 31; and promotion loss or demotion, 31-32; and "SMART" performance goals, 28; and successful progression, 29-30
"managing up", 28-29
manufacturing, and innovation, 2-3
Mark, Mitchell, 74
Marlin Company, 74
McConnell, Edwinia A., 25
McNeill, Corbin A., Jr., 29
McNeil Pharmaceutical Company, 65
McNerney, W. James, 98
Medical Group Management Association, 51
medical model, 40-41
Medical Practice Management, 90
Mercer Human Resource Consulting, 93
Merchantile Bankshares, 30
Meredith, Joe S., 102
mergers and acquisitions, 59; and effect on employees, 73
Messer, Mitchell, 74
Microsoft, 49, 66-67
military model, 37-38
The Mill, 105
millennial leadership, 21, 22
Miller, Robert Steed, 69
mission statement, 24
Monitor Group, 1-2
Monroe, William, 19
Moore, Harold G., Lt. General (retired), 107-108
Moorer, Michael, 44
moral model, 1-2
Morgan, Lynn, 31-32

Morgan, Robert, 33-34, 74
Morgan, Walker and Associates, 31-32
Morin, William J., 91-92
Moses, Alexander R., 102
mothers: and influences on success, 19-20; moving in and out of workplace, 80-81
motivation: of employees, 32, 42; and groups, 39-40
Motorola, 2-3, 6
Moynihan, Dan, 93
Much, John, 30
Muller, Thomas, 100-101
multi-generational businesses, 5-6

NASA model, 38
Nasser, Jacques, 39
National Center of Health Statistics, 101
Navy Seals, 37
NBA model, 39-40
negative outcomes, planning for, 31
Nelson, Cathy, 107
nepotism, 2-3
networking, 79-80
Newman, Frank, 29
New York Historical Society, 5
New York Yankee Major League Baseball team, 38-39
Nextera Enterprises, 86
nonverbal clues, 13
Nordstrom's, 53, 67-68
Nortel Networks, 60

observation skills, 13
office design, optimum, 99-100
office guidelines, 24-26
Olian, Judy, 97-103
Olympics, 39
open communication, 97

partnerships, 59
Patterson, Floyd, 44
performance, and service and expectations, 107-108
performance goals, 28
performance model, 42-44
performance monitor, customer satisfaction as, 3
performance review, 28
performances and practices, of successful groups, 51-52
personal success. *See also* recognition; in managerial progression, 29-30
personnel development, 23-26; and career development, 23-24; and compensation and benefits, 23-24; and decision-making ability, 23-24; and desirable job attributes, 23-24; and employee contribution to success, 23-24; and job control, 23-24; and job satisfaction, 23-24; and job security, 23-24; management's concern for employees, 23-24; and mission statement, 24; and policy consistency, 23-24; and problem resolution, 23-24; and skill utilization, 23-24; and work habits, 24-26
Peter Principle, 77
Pew Charitable Trust, 76
Pitney Bowes, 78
Plante & Moran, 90-91
Polaroid Corporation, 54
policy consistency, 23-24
power, and management versus workers, 11
PPG Industries, 28
praise, 15
pregnancy, and job searching, 81-82
pride, in work, 82
problem resolution, 23-24

productivity, of groups, 37–40
professions, consumer feelings about, 85–86
promotion, losing a, 31
Public Agenda, 76
public behavior, 76
public relations, 13–15; managing, 62
public trust, restoring, 65–66
Puller, Lewis B., General, 17

Razorfish, 100–101
recognition. *See also* incentives; of achievement, 108
Reina, Dennis, 88–89
Reina, Michelle, 88–89
Reinas Consultants, 88–90
relationship, between work and home life, 99
reputation building, 62
Rhoten, Bart, 89–90
risk, 62
Roth, John, 60–61
Rowan and Blewitt, 65
rudeness, 76
"Run for the Roses", 45–46

Scott, H. Lee, 54–55
Seibel system, 41–42
service, and performance, 107–108
Shellenbarger, Sue, 87, 99
Shire Pharmaceuticals, 30
Sibson & Company, 86
six-sigma approach, 46
skills: sought by employers, 17–18; utilization of, 23–24
"SMART" performance goals, 28
Smith, Nina, 32
Soderholm, Karen, 107
Spherion Consulting Group, 33–34, 74
sports model, 38–40

spousal/boss conflict, 99
Stackteck Systems, Inc., 73
Stahel, Rolf, 30
Starr, Jacob, 6
Stern, DeWitt A., 5–6
Stern, DeWitt H., 5–6
Stern, Jolyon, 6
Stimpson, Henry, 88–89
Stout, Hilary, 33
Strauss, Benjamin, 6
stress, in the workplace. *See* employee stressors
stress avoidance behavior, 75–76
Stum, David, 87–88
success: business (*see* business success); personal (*see* personal success)
succession leadership, 21, 22
Sunbeam Corp., 54
supervisory attributes, positive, 20–21

taikomochi, 15
Takeda Pharmaceuticals Co., 13, 91
team concept, 37–40
technology: and business needs, 60; co-promotion of, 2–3; productivity-enhancing, 106
Texas A&M, 79
"The Seven Deadly Sins", 2–3
"the sins of premature entrepreneurialship", 33
thoroughbred horse racing, 45–46
Todd, Paula, 93
Toothman Rice, 21
"Top Gun Techniques", 37–38
Towers Perrin, 92–94
Trotter, Lloyd, 32
trust and betrayal, in the workplace, 87–90
Trust and Betrayal in the Workplace, 88–89

"trust model", 88-90
turnover, rates and costs of employee, 86-87
Tuzman, Kaleil, 33
Tyco International, 54
Tylenol™, 65
Tyson, Mike, 44

unemployed colleagues, advice for, 79-80
Union Pacific Railroad, 102
United States Marine Corps, 17
University of Michigan Business School, American Society, 53

Valancy, Jack, 90
values and ideals, of leadership, 97
verbal cues, 13-14
Viagene™, 40-41
violence, in the workplace, 74
visionary leadership, 21, 22
volunteerism, 82
Vukmir, Rade B., MD, JD: background and career of, v-vi, "About the Author" section; and *The Mill*, 105

Wachner, Linda, 68
Wadsworth, Borhl, Dr., 76
The Wall Street Journal, 79-80
Wal-Mart, 54-55
Walton, Sam, 54-55
Wang, Henry, 9
Warnaco Group, 68
Waste Management, Inc., 69
Watson Wyatt Worldwide, 87-88
Web Trends™, 32

Welch, Jack, 19
wellness benefits and plans, 102-103
West Virginia Wellness Network, 102
Wexner, Leslie, 67
What Every Successful Woman Knows, 12 Breakthrough Strategies to Get Power and Ignite Your Career, 91-92
The While Collar Sweat Shop and Deterioration of Work and its Rewards in Corporate America, 105
"Why People Lie" concept, 1-2
Woolworth, Frank Winfield, 6
work environments: best "business practice" companies and, 99-103; and employee stressors (*see* employee stressors)
work habits, 24-26
workplace efficiency, 75-76
workplace stress. *See* employee stressors
workplace stress avoidance behavior, 75-76. *See also* employee stressors
workplace violence, 74
work rules, of Albert Einstein, 1

Yankelovich Monitor, 78-79
Yuzo Koyama, 15

Zaslo, Jeffrey, 79-80
Zguris, Tom, MD, MBA, 107
Zimmel, Alisa, 13, 91-92
Zook, Chris, 55-56

About the Author

Rade B. Vukmir, MD, JD is president of Critical Care Medicine Associates, a medical service and consulting enterprise. He is trained in emergency medicine and critical care medicine, and has a legal degree with a specialization in health law.

This company has been successful over the last thirteen years providing a wide variety of clinical medical activity, education, medicolegal services, and business consultation services.

In addition, Dr. Vukmir has authored over two-dozen journal articles. Previous publications include *Care of the Critically Ill* (Parthenon Press) and *Airway Management in the Critically Ill* (Parthenon Press) in the medical genre.

Dr. Vukmir has also published a novel in its third printing and a historical nonfiction work entitled *The Mill* (Rowman and Littlefield Co.). This latter work addresses the changing business environment of an aging steel industry and its impact on the day-to-day lives of the inhabitants of its once thriving industrial town.

This latest work, *Lessons Learned: Successful Management in a Changing Marketplace* attempts to unite a wide variety of work experience and business principals offered by the author and others in the field. This is to both illuminate the business development pathway for those nearer to the field, as well as to provide a healthy introspective review for the more experienced entrepreneur.

"Recognition is the cure for many ills."
Kuhn

www.ingramcontent.com/pod-product-compliance
Lightning Source LLC
Chambersburg PA
CBHW020806160426
43192CB00006B/467